A Country Doctor's Casebook

MIDWEST 🎇 REFLECTIONS

MEMOIRS AND PERSONAL HISTORIES
OF THE PEOPLE OF THE UPPER MIDWEST

A Country Doctor's Casebook

TALES FROM THE NORTH WOODS

Roger A. MacDonald, M.D.

Foreword by Roger Welsch

BOREALIS
BOOKS

Publication of this book was supported in part by the George W. Neilson Fund.

Borealis Books is an imprint of the Minnesota Historical Society Press

www.borealisbooks.org

The Minnesota Historical Society Press is a member of the Association of American University Presses.

Manufactured in the United States of America

10 9 8 7 6 5 4 3 2 1

♾ The paper used in this publication meets the minimum requirements of the American National Standard for Information Sciences—Permanence for Printed Library materials, ANSI Z39.48-1984.

International Standard Book Number
0-87351-474-2

Library of Congress Cataloging-in-Publication Data

MacDonald, Roger Allan, 1924–

A country doctor's casebook : tales from the north woods / Roger Allan MacDonald ; foreword by Roger Welsch.

    p.   cm.

ISBN 0-87351-474-2 (alk. paper)

1. MacDonald, Roger Allan, 1924–
2. Physicians—Minnesota—
   Biography.
3. Medicine, Rural—Minnesota.
I. Title.

R153 .M33 2002

610′.92—dc21

                    2002004319

"Debbie" originally appeared in the publication *Never Like You Plan: An Anthology of Writing by Elder Minnesotans* (COMPAS: Community Programs in the Arts, St. Paul, 1994).

A Country Doctor's Casebook

Foreword

W HEN EXACTLY *is* history? A hundred years ago? Before
World War II? Before Dad? That may seem like a trivial,
even silly question, and yet it is one that is worth considering
simply because we usually don't think about it. The fact of the
matter is, history is right now. It is happening at this very moment. And not just to "important" people, but to you and people like you.

Roger MacDonald knows this. He has had the wisdom to
realize that his own work in northern Minnesota as a rural doctor constitutes not just history, but important history and,
more significantly, interesting history. What's even better, Dr.
MacDonald has been generous enough to write down and
share that history with us.

I have long argued that here in the middle of the continent
we are still, in fact, on the frontier. Yes, I know: your town has cel-
ebrated its centennial, maybe even its bicentennial, and is way,
way too old to be thought of as "the frontier." Tell that to a German who lives in a village through which a two-thousand-year-
old Roman road passes, or to a Dane in whose church there are
Viking images carved a millennium ago, or to a Pueblo Indian
who can point across the plaza to the rock that plugs the hole

through which human beings clambered up from the Under-
world to become his own forefathers.

Nor is the recency of our time-line only a matter of relativ-
ity. I believe you can gain some sense of your remarkably short
tenure in your geography by watching the local evening news.
Or more precisely, the local weather forecast. When the meteor-
ologist lists the record lows and highs for the day, what are the
dates? 1936? Well, that's not very long ago, is it? Jeez, I was *born*
in 1936.

How often does your local station inform you that today you
enjoyed a new record high, or low, or wind speed, or day of
drought? Once a year? Every other year? If you live somewhere
west of the Appalachians, I'm betting you experience an ex-
pansion of your knowledge of what is possible in your location
every few weeks, maybe every month. Even a new weather mile-
stone every couple of months indicates—at least to me—that
we are still trying to figure out exactly how wide the parameters
of our geography can be, and that very innocence suggests that
we simply have not been here very long. Not very long at all.

Can Roger MacDonald possibly tell us anything about frontier medicine? He's still alive. He began his practice right after
World War II. *I* remember World War II, and I'm just a kid!
Well, okay, maybe I'm not a kid, but would I ever be considered
a frontiersman? Read Roger MacDonald's stories of his long
experience in rural, backwoods Minnesota—on Indian reservations and in remote, isolated areas—and you will know that
he can tell us plenty about frontier medicine. What's more, at
the incredible rate medical science changed in the second half
of the twentieth century, anyone who was in the field twenty
years ago can tell stories that would chill the new internist's
heart. So, was Roger MacDonald a frontier doctor, a pioneer?
Get this: *he went on house calls!*

MacDonald provides us a unique view of people we might not otherwise meet in the pages of history. For one thing, everyone eventually needs medical attention, so MacDonald's experiences cover the full range of humanity. Moreover, he constitutes an educated, insightful element within his geography just as any doctor does, but to our good fortune he is also an unusually articulate narrator and sensitive observer. His stories are not just interesting to read but moving, sometimes hilarious—again, a reflection of the range of human experience.

It is not simply a matter of MacDonald telling us about medical practices of long ago—in medicine fifty years *is* a long time ago—he also deals with a part of society that is not often explored in modern examinations: rural, agricultural, Native, geographically remote. Despite the homogenization of modern society with national television, super highways, and the web, remarkable gulfs persist between American urban, mainstream culture and rural, backwoods life, and some of us find real delight and perspective in those differences.

As I read MacDonald's stories, I can't help but think of my own experiences at the edge of Nebraska's vast and sparsely populated Sandhills. There is an attitude in the village I call home, an understanding that outsiders might not immediately grasp but that is not the least bit subtle. An example: A few weeks ago I was entering our local grocery store when the proprietor's miserable, yappy, obnoxious dog came along. I greeted him in a friendly way. I love dogs, even pseudo-dogs like this one, and besides, he was way too little to do a big lug like me any harm. Or so I thought.

It is of course precisely that kind of hubris that inspires little boogers like this one to tear into a grown man's pant leg—which this one did—rip it off, and then take a Milkbone-sized divot out of the well-wisher's leg—which this one also did. I limped into the grocery store, cussing the wretched cur, and asked Kerry, the owner, if his damn dog's shots were current. Without so much as looking up to see my shredded clothing and bleeding calf, he said, "Naw, Rog, he hasn't had any shots, but that dog has bitten a lot of people recently and none of them got sick, so you're probably going to be all right." Being insensitive, I have never thought to follow up on the dog's health. I submit that this is probably not the way the victim, the dog owner, or for that matter the dog would behave in an urban setting.

Roger MacDonald has not only spent a lifetime working in a context like this, he has brought compassion, humor, courage, and technology to it. And what's even better, in the following pages he has taken the time and care to tell us about his adventures in frontier medicine, and to do it well. Don't read past this page unless you have some time to spare. You're not going to put this book down very soon.

ROGER WELSCH

Acknowledgments

THESE REMINISCENCES are dedicated to those who handed me their well-being to hold in trust; to those health professionals with whom I was privileged to work for such a long time; to colleagues who have also experienced the joys—and anxieties—of an isolated rural practice; to friends who still share this wonderful land in which we live; to my family, who endured the nearly impossible restrictions of living with a solo physician. Thank you Mary, Bruce, Tom, Pamela, Jane, and Allan.

To mentors Dr. Arthur Wells, M.D., for whom medical practice and scientific integrity were synonymous, and Dr. Ralph Hanover, M.D., who taught me so much; to Dr. Carl Wall, M.D., whose life displayed such graciousness; to Dr. David Hilfiker, M.D., Dr. Barbara Bank, M.D., and Dr. Michael Debevec, M.D., for demonstrating that today's physicians have picked up the torch.

A special thanks to editor Shannon M. Pennefeather, whose patience, tact, and expertise have made this journey into the past a pleasant one.

And, most especially, these stories are dedicated to Barbara MacDonald, who was there.

A Country Doctor's Casebook

Introduction

FOR THIRTY-SEVEN YEARS, beginning in 1948, I practiced frontline medicine in northernmost Minnesota. The north country and its friendship with nature appealed to me from the start. I had graduated from the University of Minnesota Medical School in 1946, then spent a year as an intern at St. Luke's Hospital in Duluth, Minnesota. One day in August, my roommate, Ed Zupanc, and I studied a map of Minnesota, looking for the largest patch of white, roadless area it displayed. We hitchhiked 165 miles to the northwest from Duluth on an exploratory expedition.

As it happened, Ed chose a different career, but on January 7, 1948, I joined an experienced and enormously busy general practitioner, whom I'll call Samuel Hargrave, M.D.

I had met my wife, Barbara Bramer, while serving my internship. A registered nurse working in the delivery room, she combined skill with dark beauty, courtesy of a generous dash of Ojibwe genes. (I found an extra month of training in obstetrics to be attractive.) During many of my years in practice we worked shoulder to shoulder.

My life was busy, productive, satisfying—and at times overwhelming. In the city, a patient can select a doctor by category:

a woman in labor does not seek out an orthopedist. If someone arrives at the office with a rare disease, a "fascinoma" in slangy medical jargon, a colleague versed in the problem is usually available on a doctor's own hospital staff. In a solo practice more than one hundred miles from the nearest specialist, patients with *any* conceivable affliction may come to the office or emergency room. A disastrously ill or injured person, arriving in the middle of the night, tries the courage and perceptiveness of a lone physician.

A country doctor comes to know the people she or he cares for so intimately. As a woman once told me, she considered the doctor to be almost a member of the family. Patients become friends and friends become patients. These relationships can be both therapeutic and perilous, for detachment and cool judgment in a crisis are essential to both patient and physician. Allow me to illustrate this dilemma with an example.

Frank was a friend whom I had been privileged to help wrestle the devil of addiction. He had learned to live without alcohol, if not tobacco. He had a heart attack at a time when our ability to change its outcome was limited. For a couple of days Frank did as well as his injured heart would allow. Then, an arrest. A damaged heart can slip into electrical chaos when impulses to keep it beating cancel each other out. I had just gotten home for supper when he crashed. It took me four or five minutes to return to the hospital. Members of the nursing staff were doing what they were well trained to do: cardiac massage, breathing for him, using oxygen. I joined the team: objective, clicking off the necessary procedures, giving requisite drugs, defibrillating electrically.

We worked for half an hour. I remained the trained clinician

I needed to be while working on "a case." Eventually the time came, as it ever must, when I, as physician, had to say, enough. Cease resuscitation attempts. The battle is lost.

I said it, and on the instant fell into my role as Frank's friend, with all my sealed-off grief released in an explosion of tears. His wife and I huddled in the waiting room until we had shared our private requiem.

So how did I separate emotion from the detached professionalism my alma mater had nurtured? Actually, I don't know. We doctors cope as best we can, each in his or her own way.

It had not occurred to me to wonder if a pioneer considered himself to be one. Then one day a historian contacted me to ask what medicine had been like in "the old days." Reminiscing is something we seniors do well, so I was glad to oblige. Write down some of my tales? But a doctor is pledged to confidentiality: my patients were special and I hold their welfare in trust. Change names, combine features of two or more cases, fuzz up details to obscure identities? Think about it, she said.

I have. These stories are the result. I practiced in two different areas, both near Ojibwe reservations, but let me make them one. These towns were as northern as a Minnesotan can claim, so I'll call my town Northpine. Because of the glorious egalitarianism among the people of northern Minnesota, I had quickly become known, and addressed, as "RAM" (my initials), or, when circumstances dictated a more formal approach, as "Doc." Mutual respect was never a casualty. I offer these stories as a tribute to my Northpine neighbors, who handed me their well-being to hold in trust.

Justice in the Wild, Wild North

R HEUMATIC FEVER results from the body's attempt to fight off the bacterium we doctors call Beta-hemolytic Streptococcus, "Strep throat." Immunity runs amok, and misguided defense systems attack tissues that are vital to life. By a more rapid conquest of the organism, penicillin prevents this breakdown in the immune system. Unfortunately—from a youngster's point of view—in 1948 "penicillin" and "shot" were synonymous.

As the only doctor for miles, I was sometimes forced into the uncomfortable position of having to treat my own children. Once I had to give my son Bruce, then aged four or five, a shot of penicillin. I laid down the used syringe and turned to say something to my wife. He picked it up and jabbed it authoritatively, needle-first, into my knee. When I yelped, he patted my leg and said, "There, there, Dad. Don't cry."

Trillium was a village some fifty-five miles from Northpine. There was no doctor closer than I. In an attempt to fill the void, I traveled to Trillium twice a week. My "office" was a front upstairs room of the Buena Vista Hotel.

One day Master Abner Harding, aged ten, arrived at my office with a sore throat and the inability to readily swallow that characterizes Strep. I did my dastardly deed, giving the lad his injection into a buttock tight as a weight lifter's biceps. He fled to the safety of the hallway that served as a waiting area, hitching up his britches as he went.

I sat down next to the boy's father. Young Abner stood in front of me, thoughtfully rubbing his behind. I said, "John, your boy's tonsillitis looks like Strep, so I gave him penicillin."

Abner gazed at me intently from an eye-level vantage. Without warning, he delivered a splendid right hook to my chin. Then Abner turned sprinter, escaping down the broad steps of the hotel and out the front door. John followed more sedately, propriety strangling on laughter that would not be denied.

I rubbed my jaw. Justice in the wild, wild north can be terrible and swift.

House Call

I T WAS THE THIRD MONTH of my shiny new rural medical practice. The doorbell to my rented apartment rang. I threw open the door, letting in blustery March weather, Northpine-style. I stared at a huddled figure standing on the brief porch. The man's chin bore proof that shaving was an occasional event, and about his mouth wiry bristles were white with frost. He wore a limp cap of faded plaid. Frazzled flaps barely covered the tips of his ears and the bill drooped, causing him to peer from under its overhang. He spoke in a creaky voice.

"You the new doc what comes to Trillium?"

I identified myself as Dr. MacDonald and confessed that I did indeed travel twice a week to hold office hours in the village named for a northern wildflower. "You are?"

"McNabb," he growled. "Come with me." The slightly built man staggered when he turned away and limped toward my new Ford, parked beside the house. He crawled into the passenger seat. I hollered, "Hey, Mister—Oh, shoot." I waded through snow and yanked open the car door. "What do you want?"

"A doc," he said.

"What for?"

"My wife."

"Where is she?"

"Home. Hurry up."

I glared at the unusual Mr. McNabb, then returned to the

house, pulled on a hooded jacket and chopper mitts, grabbed my proud new medical case, and stomped back into winter's briskness. My car now reeked with essence of McNabb.

"What's wrong with your wife?" I demanded.

"Stuck."

"Stuck! Where?"

"Home! Get a-goin'. She needs the doc."

I turned the ignition key. "Where to?"

"I'll show ya."

"In general where?"

"Hard by Trillium."

A Sunday afternoon. Fifty-five miles.

I drove steadily, covertly studying my passenger. "Tell me again what's wrong with your wife."

"Stuck."

"McNabb, I need information."

"You'll see."

I decided to establish a beachhead into the realm of broader communication. "Your name sounds Irish."

"'Tis."

"Have you lived in Trillium long?"

"Don't live there, never have."

"But you said—"

"Hard *by* Trillium."

"Have you lived hard by Trillium long?"

"No."

"Where are you from, before hard by—before?"

"East."

"Where east?"

"Pennsylvania."

"Where in Penns—Oh, crap."

"No, hard by Altoona."

The man dozed off and we rode in silence. Trillium's water tower loomed above the trees. "Now where to?" I asked. McNabb jerked a thumb back over his shoulder. I skidded to a stop on the frozen highway. "What do you mean?" I repeated the gesture.

"You went by the turnoff."

"Where!"

"Last crossroad."

I all but grabbed the guy by the front of his jacket. "Listen, you, give! Where are we going and what in tarnation is wrong with your wife?"

"Baby."

"Her baby is sick?"

"No! It's stuck."

"Do you mean she's having a *baby?*"

"Like I said: stuck."

"McNabb, I'm not prepared for a delivery!"

He looked at me disdainfully. "You a doc, ain't you?"

"But not a magician." I glared at McNabb and sat back to think. Then I restarted the car and drove on into Trillium, where I raided my tiny office of all its sterile supplies. The silence that now lay between us was cold as the fist of winter around us, broken only by frozen-metal squeaks from the car frame, the muted crunch of tires pulling through snow. Eventually McNabb ordered a halt at a spot along the narrow wilderness road no different from hundreds of others to my jaundiced eye. I dragged my scanty hoard of supplies from the car and said to McNabb, "You take—"

There was no sign of the limping Irishman.

"McNabb!"

A desolate swamp forest of black spruces and tamaracks echoed my bellow. I saw no buildings. McNabb reappeared, one hundred feet off the road, standing on a trail that was a waist-deep rut in the snow.

I snarled, "Oh, sure, having disposed of the easy part of the trip. How far?"

"Thirty rods."

I floundered through drifts to catch up. "Here, dang it, you carry some of this stuff." Our safari plunged into the depths of the frozen quagmire.

A forlorn log house with a dilapidated roof, a window paned equally with cardboard and glass, walls moldering from their humid surroundings. I followed my guide into a room cluttered with shabby furniture, a frigid space that was kitchen, dining room, and living room. The sour odor of smoky wood fires competed with an aroma of humanity that I have always equated with poverty.

McNabb darted to the doorway of a second room and peered around the jamb, then stomped to a rusty wood range in one corner and prepared to light a fire. He nodded curtly in the direction of the other room.

The woman was younger than her husband by a decade. She lay quietly on a homemade bed against the wall of a cramped room devoid of adornment. Grimy and solemn, she watched me over the top of a tattered blanket, held to cover the lower half of her face. She jumped at my movements, alert as a deer of the forest, trembling when I approached. Something white lay over her in streaks and piles. I touched a patch. Snow! I looked around and saw daylight between some of the logs. I pulled up the blanket from the foot of the bed.

Limp, flaccid, dusky, from between the woman's thighs protruded the lower half of a baby. I knelt urgently and touched the cold little body. "How long?"

"Last evening," she whispered.

"Lady, push for me, see if you can . . . good. It moved. Again. Here it comes. Once more . . . there! And the afterbirth is ready, too."

No bleeding, no obvious infection, the mother apparently all right. Incredible. I wrapped the dead baby in a towel, squeezed the woman's uterus through her now-soft abdomen, and covered her again with the blanket. I brushed snow onto the floor and sat heavily on the edge of the bed. "I'm sorry. It was a boy. You knew?"

She dipped her chin. McNabb appeared at the bedroom door, hobbled awkwardly to her side and patted her shoulder.

"Why didn't you get help?" I asked.

"Did," he said. "Got you."

"But, yesterday? What took so long?"

"Walked."

"To *Northpine?*"

"I left at nine o'clock, walked all night. I'm lamed, can't walk fast."

I heard an eerie ringing in my ears. Looked around, back at the man. A tear traced a single rivulet through the stubble on his cheek. A head held high, a steady eye.

I did my doctor things, checked Mrs. McNabb's uterus a last time and touched her shoulder.

Mr. McNabb followed me into the kitchen. He held out two quart-sized Mason jars filled with some obscure material.

"Here," he said.

"What's this?" I asked.

"Venison. Your fee. Or would three be best?"

I took the jars. "No, Mister McNabb, this is my exact fee. I thank you." We shook hands. "I'll stop to see your wife on my next trip to Trillium. No, no, that's included in my regular charge. Good day, sir."

Mr. McNabb nodded.

Emergency

OPERATOR LOIS MACINTOSH was Northpine's Ma Bell. She ran the telephone system from a switchboard in a back room of the Aristocrat Hotel (*rooms by the night or week*). So that Lois could get a day off now and then, her sister Elsie helped out. Service came on at 7:00 A.M. when Lois arrived for work and ended at 9:00 P.M. when she pulled the plug. She was prompt, especially on the evening end of things.

Having no telephones at night was both good and bad. You had to be reasonably sick to call out a doctor after hours when you had to go farther than he did.

Lois served as my answering service. If I had been out of touch for a while, I'd ring her up and ask, "Anything happening, Lois?" She'd say, "The hospital called," or "Eddie Thompson wants you. He lives across the river, that Thompson. And—" You get the idea. Nowadays you have to pay someone buckets to do half as good a job of keeping track.

One evening my telephone jangled. Lois Macintosh's voice bristled with importance. "Emergency coming in, Doc. Pete Flaubert. He told Edna at the hospital to have a doctor waiting. He's from Trillium, isn't he? Called from there. Want me to connect you with the hospital?"

"Thanks, Lois. One-five."

"I know the number, Doc." I listened to a ring from the near end. She asked, "How was the stew tonight at Woody's Café?"

"Good, Lois."

"I might run in after work. I hate cooking so late at—Hello, Edna, here's Doc. Don't talk long, now. It's nearly nine and I'll be closing down."

I heard no click; Lois was fulfilling her role as community monitor.

When I arrived breathless at the hospital, nurse Edna Freeman asked if there was anything else I wanted prepared. I finger-tallied: "Suture tray, cast material, ready in lab and x-ray, a blood donor on tap. I wish you had asked Peter Flaubert the nature of his emergency." I glanced at my watch again and imagined a car speeding toward us along that cold slash of lonely highway. Five miles out? Someone in agony! Bleeding? Perhaps labor.

I said, "Maybe we should set up in the delivery room." Edna rolled her eyes. She snapped on lights with unusual vigor.

Mr. Peter Flaubert never came.

The next time I went to Trillium, I used the telephone. "Is this Peter Flaubert?"

A voice said, "Could be. What'd you want?"

"I'm Dr. MacDonald. When you didn't show up—"

"Who?"

"Dr. MacDonald. You called the other night—"

"I don't know anyone named MacDonald."

"The doctor," I said.

He snorted. "There's no doctor in Trillium. Well, 'cept that young pup what comes over from Northpine."

"That's me, I'm the young—Uh, I'm Dr. MacDonald."

"Oh, that one."

"I've been wondering what your emergency was. Worried, in fact."

"I got no emergency."

"But you called the hospital in Northpine."

"Oh, that. By the time me and the boys finished chores, we decided it was too late to drive so far. I'm a working man and—"

I chewed words hot as jalapeño peppers . . . and swallowed them.

The lesson? In the words of that famous military cliché, "Wait until you see the whites of their eyes."

We Work Not Alone

WORKING WITH an experienced general practitioner was a glorious chance to learn management of a rural practice, almost an apprenticeship. Then, after three-and-a-half years, Dr. Sam Hargrave moved to the neighboring town of Koochiching. His long-term office nurse, Marsha Edgerton, went with him. I was left to run the hospital, my wife, R.N. Barbara MacDonald, to supervise its staff. I needed someone to work in the office.

Ready-made paramedical professionals clustered in places like Duluth and Minneapolis. During a visit to my internship-alma mater, St. Luke's Hospital in Duluth, I caught up with medical technologist Vera Thrommald.

"I'm the doctor your supervisor mentioned to you," I said.

"Yes, from someplace up north."

"I've been told that you intend to work where your efforts will really matter."

Vera Thrommald's eyes flashed and her chin quivered. "There are so many unfortunates who need help. Jesus has called me to his banner."

"Wonderful! A mission. That's what I want to discuss with you."

"Africa," she sighed.

"I can appreciate your feelings—"

"South America."

"—because in a sort of way, I feel the same. Now, Northpine badly needs—"

"Where's that?"

"The place up north you mentioned."

Her eyes lost their glaze of distant visions. "Minnesota?"

"Yes, 165 miles northwest of Duluth."

"Oh no!" She shook her head and a lock of hair fell across her forehead. "Too remote."

"But—"

"It's nice to meet you, Doctor."

"Mission," I squeaked.

"Bye-bye." She smiled bewitchingly.

Elaine Andresen perched on the edge of the client's chair in my office, prim and tense, hands held prayerfully in her lap. Her breath came in tight gasps. My smile was of the "everything will be all right" variety as I asked, "What can I do for you today, Mrs. Andresen?"

She glanced at me, then down at her hands. She straightened and raised her chin. I played my medical game of "which way are we going?"

Female problems?

She said, "I'm not really sick, Doctor."

Reassess. Family troubles? What was her husband's name?

"What I came for . . ." She pursed her lips. I studied her face. Strong features, accustomed to smiling—I knew that from our contacts at Meinert's Market, where she worked.

"I was wondering, would you need . . ." My medical guessing game hit a dead end. ". . . an office girl?"

I traded my smile for a look of appraisal. Tall. Pleasant. "Yes, indeed. Someone versatile."

"Like Marsha Edgerton," she said. She stood up. "This is preposterous. I had no business coming like this."

"We might consider the possibility."

"I have no skills. I can't nurse or do lab work, have never seen an x-ray machine. I keep my husband's books, but that's just arithmetic."

I said, "You present your credentials in an unusual manner."

"Oh, Doctor, I would study and learn all I could."

"How old are you?"

"Thirty-six."

"Your education?"

"Just—just high school."

"The job would be demanding."

She drew herself up and her gaze went straight to mine. "I'm not afraid to work."

"When can you begin?"

"Are you offering me a job?"

"I believe I'll ask Barbara to make a nurse of you first, although I'm getting dang tired of doing my own labs and x-rays."

Elaine was a quick study. She learned to scrub as a surgical nurse, do blood counts and simple chemistries, and take x-rays. Oh yes, she did my bookwork, too. I'm fairly certain Miss Thrommald would not have done that.

The Rez

CHIPPEWA LAKE was a reservation, a town, and, indeed, a body of water, a shallow pond some four to five miles across. The name is a corruption of the word "Ojibwe," "Chippewa" being the closest pronunciation pioneer Caucasian tongues could manage. The lake was one large wild-rice paddy: rice was an important food and its sale a source of livelihood for people on the Rez.

My Ojibwe/Swedish father-in-law was a respected leader in the Minnesota Chippewa Tribe. At his urging, I had agreed to travel to this remote reservation to hold weekly "clinics." The community was fifty-five miles southeast of Northpine, reached by way of a narrow, rutted dirt road, Minnesota State Highway 65. I confess to having had trepidation that first day, as I followed the curving track under all those trees. Indianness. I had made only two visits to Barbara's parental home before our marriage. They provided little sense of what I should expect from a society so different from any I had known.

The reservation revealed itself gradually as I drove. There were no highway signs. On the right, a tarpaper shack in a small clearing amid pervasive trees. Then a pair of identical, square, white clapboard—sided houses with hip roofs rising to a point, a cubist caricature of a teepee. On the left, the skeletal remains of a sawmill: piles of sawdust, a few forlorn, weathered logs, a sketchy framework of poles still bearing a couple of corrugated-iron roof panels. A Quonset building with a hand-lettered sign before it reading "Wild Rice for Sale." An occasional side road, twin tire treads meandering out of sight toward some anonymous destination. Finally, over a slight rise in the bumpy road, the village lay before me. Small houses were placed at random, as though they had been toys scattered about by a childhood cousin of Paul Bunyan. A co-op store, fugitive from a movie western. A white church with a New England steeple. The schoolhouse.

A delegation of three men met me at the elementary school, which was a square white box of a building. Foxy Bronson, teacher: Caucasian. Frank Brown, reservation Indian agent: his copper skin and rotund shape attested to a Native heritage. Bill Makos, elder of the Chippewa Lake Band of Minnesota Chippewas: the man stood straight and proud.

Barbara and I became friends with Foxy and his wife, Beatrice, by dint of proximity. They were teachers, and the only "office space" available on the Rez was a small landing inside the back door of the school. Half staircases led up and down from it. We cavalierly locked the outside door—no fire marshal had visited the school during Foxy's twelve-year tenure—and hung a curtain across the "up" stairway, where the classrooms were located.

Supplies and equipment for my upstairs-downstairs "office" were limited to the bare minimum by parsimonious policy of the BIA, the Bureau of Indian Affairs. My examination table was an iron monstrosity minus one of its four legs; I propped up the relic with encyclopedias published in 1898, cast-offs courtesy of the Minneapolis Public Library. The instruments provided were rusty from disuse.

. . .

I stood in my quasi office that first morning among cartons of medical supplies, sorting what I had garnered from the Bureau of Indian Affairs Hospital in Cass Lake, Minnesota. A girl appeared at the top of the "up" stairway, six or seven in age, solemn, her hair glistening in a shaft of sunlight peeping through a dusty window. Glints of blue gleamed among those black strands. Her skin was a copper hue. A pixie. She plopped onto the top step, her gaze following my every move.

"'Cha doin'?" she asked.

"Putting things away."

"Why?"

"I'm a doctor and I need to know where things are."

"But, why?"

"Why. To be able to—Uh, what's your name?"

"Patti."

"What grade are you in?"

"Second."

"Aren't you supposed to be in class?"

"Yeah, but, I haf' to go number one." She isolated a pudgy index finger from its neighbors and waved it imploringly. "But I saw you."

"What do you like best about school?"

She rested her chin on "number one" finger, registered reflection as faithfully as Rodin's *The Thinker*.

"Lunch."

"Won't they miss you now?"

"No, but—Yes, but...but...we're having reading and I don't like that. Mrs. Bronson makes us all take turns. Phillip talks when I'm reading and she gets mad at him and makes him stop. 'Right now!' she says, only she sounds louder than Phillip. Big people can talk loud."

She jiggled in sudden excitement. "Know what? Me an' my sisters, we finally got a little brother last week. An', an' Mama says, 'Thank God, now I don't have to have any more babies.'"

A bell jangled in the corridor. Miss Patti jumped to her feet. "Oh, it's time for lunch."

Her face was an explosion of joy. For a magical moment she poised on the pinions of flight, that marvel of our species, a child. She hitched up ragged leotards and ran down the hallway to join a stampede of her classmates, her hair a lustrous flag.

Children's Christmas pageants have always seemed to me barely a notch above a session at your friendly dentist's office. One year Barbara and I were invited to stay after clinic and attend one put on by the Chippewa Lake Elementary School. We sat in honored seats near the front of the basement cafeteria in the schoolhouse, the only space large enough for such an extravaganza. The place was already steamy hot. I sighed, pondering my impending martyrdom.

A pair of bed sheets had been stitched together to serve as a curtain, hiding the kitchen and area designated "stage." It fluttered suddenly: show time, magic time. Someone hidden from sight pulled on the rope that was supposed to draw it aside. It merely wiggled. A voice that sounded remarkably like that of Foxy Bronson when coping with a behavior problem in class commented on its putative heritage. The curtain fell in a heap; Foxy made his escape into the kitchen, under cover.

An angel choir led off: first- and second-graders. I wasn't sure what song was intended, but it sounded Christmassy. Precarious halos and gauzy wings created authenticity. My "upstairs" friend Patti spied me. She waved, all her fingers at once. Her smile was as enchanting as ever.

Adeline Dubois and Cissy Portier marched front and center to recite *The Night Before Christmas*. Eight-year-old Adeline started things off. She was a waif: fatherless, her mother shackled to beer; pinched of face; her limbs skin, bone, and wisps of muscle. No childhood plumpness. Her dress, with its uneven hem, was twice handed down. She lisped through the gap in her front teeth, shared wistful yearnings for stockings filled with wonders. Cissy took over the recitation at the point when reindeer landed on the roof. Her enthusiasm and eloquence were so persuasive that more than one of us glanced up at the ceiling.

The manger scene came next. Mary was played by sixth-grader Margo Little Frog. Joseph strode down the aisle, his worn tennis shoes squeaking like a troop of mice, and resolutely arraigned himself next to the shepherds. "Get over here," Mary snapped, the gleam in her Madonna eyes boding ill for Joe, on- or off-stage.

One of the wise men knocked over a pasteboard cow. (Paper towels shined defiantly through its black-and-white hide.) The youngster wrestled it upright, then fled down the aisle to his mother.

Irene Basswood sang "Silent Night," once in English, again in Ojibwe. The girl's voice was like the haunting croon of Goodman's clarinet when he was at his most introspective.

Lex Bullhead ended the production by reciting the Lord's Prayer in Ojibwe.

It happened that kindly ladies from three of the churches in Northpine had adopted the children at Chippewa Lake, to the extent of buying and wrapping gifts for the party. Barbara and I had brought them with us: Claus Enterprises, Transportation

Division. As our personal contribution, she and I had brought two large containers of ice cream.

It was time for Santa!

Tossing off "Ho-ho-hos!" along with pieces of hard candy, St. Nick staggered down the aisle under the weight of a sack—very similar to a pillowcase—bulging with packages. To my skeptical ear, Santa sounded for all the world like James Squint-eye. (The man's title was school custodian. In truth, he was an innovative magician whose genius kept the place functioning. Every institution needs someone like him.) White chin whiskers kept slipping up over his mouth. Since Indians have the good fortune not to bear genes for facial hair, he had no practical experience in coping with shrubbery.

To the children, there was no doubt as to Santa's authenticity. Arriving at the front of the room, he delved into his bag of mystery. Beaming and strutting or shy and hesitant before such a marvel, children filed past James. Santa. The pillowcase—sack—shrank upon itself until . . .

Three children waited while Santa dived headfirst into the bag. When he popped back out his eyes were as round as those of the children, they wondering aloud what they were about to receive.

Barbara beckoned to Jim. She took three precious packages from her purse, red and green and silver. Thankful for her foresight, Santa crossed himself and accepted them.

The ledger balanced.

Epidemic

E STABLISHMENT OF Minnesota's Indian reservations during the nineteenth century was based on two principles: admittedly something had to be done with those Native Americans who had survived "civilizing," and corralling them in remote areas of no obvious commercial value kept them out of sight.

Chippewa Lake Reservation was such a place. Its inhabitants turned inward, enduring isolation, poverty, and neglect for more than one hundred years. A "system" grew up to provide needed services. Water? Drill three hand-pump wells near the center of town. After all, hauling water in buckets was good enough for Grandmama, and wasn't it a shame that one of the wells turned out to harbor typhoid organisms? Better seal that one off. Health care? Put Indian hospitals where they would be convenient—for health officials, of course.

So what was the fate of these people in the mid-twentieth century? Perhaps a story might give a hint.

The word *epidemic* raises visions of a blindly indifferent and implacable enemy. In the year 1956, add the word *poliomyelitis*—polio—and fear sinks deep its fangs. During the summer of 1956 the Salk vaccine against polio was scarce and expensive. The BIA provided none for my clinics.

August ushered in the polio season. Monica Loon Feather was my first case. Irritability, fever, a stiff and sore neck—the signs were there. A spinal tap confirmed presence of a viral meningitis, with polio the leading contender. I sent blood and stool cultures to the Minnesota Department of Health for confirmation. Within the week Todd Strongbody and Lisa Moose arrived at Northpine Hospital. Lisa's face drooped, unusual as an isolated sign of polio. Their spinal taps were positive. The second week I saw three more cases, the Makos girls and Tom Dahlman. During week three a dozen children arrived.

The people at Chippewa Lake confronted a capricious enemy invisible to the eye. From what should they hide, and behind what barrier?

By this time, someone at the BIA decided that my ranting just maybe perhaps meant a problem might exist. With help from the county health department, they commandeered a supply of vaccine. I spent a day in Chippewa Lake giving wholesale injections in accordance with the venerable doctrine of "too little, too late."

Our tiny institution in Northpine became a polio hospital. Then somebody at the state department of health noticed all my positive cultures and a Dr. Heinrich telephoned one day. "What's going on up there?" he boomed into my ear. I explained.

Dr. Heinrich joined me, and for two days we scoured the sprawling Chippewa Lake Reservation and gave Salk vaccine to anyone who had escaped my previous efforts. Indian agent Frank Brown, himself a full-blooded Ojibwe, was my interpreter. I can only imagine what ingenuity it must have taken to persuade folks as regal as Amos Geshick or Phinneas Basswood to poop in the little bottle and send it off to Minneapolis.

The long summer dragged on. I performed spinal taps every day. Most of the tests were positive. Wilbur Squinteye became paralyzed in his left leg, and I sent him to a regional hospital where he could receive the Sister Kenny method of treatment. Three more children developed a drooping facial weakness as the only manifestation of the disease. Dr. Heinrich was, well, not delighted—he was too kind a man for that. Intrigued. Doctors light up over such medical oddities.

September arrived, with its less-humid days and frosty nights. The epidemic waned, and I was called on to do spinal taps only once or twice a week. Dr. Heinrich returned and we totaled up the score.

Out of 460 Native American people, there were nineteen cases of frank polio, two with significant residual paralysis. Our four facial nerve victims recovered. Ten people without symptoms tested positive for presence of the virus, near misses.

There was a common thread among the victims of my private epidemic: all were from Chippewa Lake, and none had received timely vaccination for polio.

The "system" had failed.

To Speak the Language

THE PEOPLE AT Chippewa Lake Reservation enjoyed my attempts to speak their language. Ojibwe is an incredibly complex tongue, one perhaps never conquered except at the knee of a loving grandparent. Mrs. Adeline Porterfield attempted to teach me a few medically oriented phrases and words. (She called me *Mushkekewinini*, a "medicine man." She grinned when she said it.) Once or twice a month we'd stop at the Porterfields' after clinic, and she'd say, "Have you had supper, Doc and Barbara? We have plenty. Move over, John. A moose roast tonight. Eat up. Now, *ah-wee-see-gehen-dumina* means 'are you in pain?' *Aye-yah* is yes and *kaween* no."

I said, "*Kaween?*"

"Not quite. Halfway between a *k* and a *g*. Try again."

Many of the old people spoke no English, could not or would not. When we received a request to make a house call at a traditional home, we sent word to Frank Brown, our skilled translator.

One day Barbara, Frank, and I drove along a narrow winding road confined by snow: Amos Geshick's driveway. It dodged great boulders and detoured past trees half as wide as our car. The house nestled in a grove of pines, a bungalow sided with green roofing material.

We filed into the larger of the two rooms, inhaling a comforting aroma of wood smoke, a dash of kerosene, and an odor for which I never found a source, a nutty essence that made me think of home-tanned leather. All "Old Indian" homes I have visited have this enticing and exotic scent.

Five people sat cross-legged in a rough circle, three women and two men. There were no chairs. My stiff-jointed long legs creaked when I thought about it.

Frank Brown indicated me with his open palm.

"*Mushkekewinini* (medicine man)."

"*Boozhoo* (a greeting)." Everyone nodded and glanced politely aside. We stood uncertainly by the door. I looked at Barbara. She shrugged, a micro-twitch. Frank talked to the people in occasional quiet phrases.

I studied the Geshick family. Amos Geshick, an important name in this community. Gray hair, cut sometime in the past, not at shoulder length. Dignified, with a face to grace a postage stamp or coin. A woman across from him, his contemporary. Roundly plump. A plaid flannel shirt and jeans. Her hair was nearly white. Next, a younger version of Amos Geshick. His green Woolrich shirt stretched to contain the robustness of his frame. Her back to us, a quiet woman sat at his side. Across the circle was a young woman, late teens or early twenties. Her cheeks bore a blush that had come from a compact. She glanced at us and giggled silently into her hand.

They discoursed among themselves. Considered. Opinions were exchanged in the lilting tones and "shush" sounds of the Ojibwe language. Occasionally Frank added a comment. Amos Geshick stared straight ahead. At last he gathered the reins of debate into his own hands and spoke to Frank.

Frank chuckled with belly-shaking good humor. His eyes sparkled when he turned to me.

"Well?" I said.

"They want some aspirin."

Treatment

E VEN IN THE 1950S, the major drug-manufacturing companies were caught between their roles as profit-making organizations beholden to stockholders and their dedication to important, meaningful research. They spent millions of dollars on "samples," sending doctors boxes full of new and heavily promoted drugs "to dispense to needy patients." Never did they include standard, inexpensive, effective drugs in this largess. (My simmering quarrel with the industry never extended to the local drug store, however. The dedicated pharmacists I knew as colleagues in the northern reaches of our state were as vulnerable to the grasp of the large companies as my patients and I.)

I challenged the drug company representatives who called on me: "I have 460 patients at Chippewa Lake Reservation who rarely receive timely or adequate numbers and kinds of drugs from the Bureau of Indian Affairs. You supply me with *their* needs!"

Three representatives met the challenge, and for years I supplemented my BIA stock with their samples. I salute those three.

Many of my adventures arose when I was well away from my home office in Northpine. Chippewa Lake Reservation presented so many health challenges. Some were fairly routine: winter coughs, bronchitis, an occasional pneumonia. Barbara doled out our BIA-rationed antibiotics, our drug samples, those placebo doses of Brown's cough mix. But one January day, the parking lot was full when we arrived at the Chippewa Lake school and the hallway was jammed. While we hurriedly set up, I heard the reason.

Back in the hall some child began to cough ... and cough ... would he ever draw breath? His inhalation when it came was agonized, drawn out like a rising siren. The "whoop" of whooping cough: pertussis.

An epidemic sweeps before it all who cannot resist. Children were the victims of whooping cough, especially those under one year of age. I checked with the public health nurse. Her records indicated that there were thirty-five infants on the reservation.

I had read of giving hyperimmune serum to babies as protection. I called the state department of health and reached an old friend, Dr. Heinrich. "Right away," he boomed. "I'll send a dozen vials. Give one initially, then follow with a second in two to four days. Start as soon as possible."

I said, "I'll need a lot more than twelve."

"See how it goes. Those people don't always follow up very well."

"They will when given the chance." I ordered a second, third, and fourth dozen vials within the week.

Serum is the clear, straw-colored fluid of blood from which all clotable material and cells have been removed. It contains antibodies, bacteria-fighting proteins produced by the body. "Hyperimmune" refers to serum obtained from donors who have been rendered strongly immune by vaccination. Today we extract the important part of the serum, the gamma globulins, and give only that fraction, a volume of one-half to one cc, less than half a teaspoonful. In those days we had not yet perfected that technique, and each injection consisted of fifty cc, nearly two ounces. Picture injecting a ten- or twenty-pound baby with an ounce of serum in each tiny buttock. Twice.

We drove all over the sprawling reservation, Frank Brown, Barbara, and I. Frank was guide and translator when needed, Barbara in charge of gentle persuasion, while I, the guy behind the syringe, quickly wore out my welcome. We convinced the mothers of all thirty-five infants.

Winter spent its days, and we became accustomed to a steady chorus of whoops coming from classrooms upstairs, the aftermath of severe pertussis. The only children on the reservation who had not been ill were the babies who had received the serum. Dr. Heinrich calculated that we should have expected two, three, even four or five deaths among those tots.

This time the "system" did not fail.

Brotherly Love

I HEARD the outside door to my office open. The staircase leading upstairs was the requisite story and a half in height that customs of the time demanded. (A subtle test of cardiac capacity.) Climbing footsteps were paired and halting. A masculine voice scratchy with pre-adolescence said, "You tell 'im."

Another, a tone or so higher, said, "Dassn't. You're ta oldest."

"You begun 'er!"

"I never!" Clatter, clatter downstairs.

"Ma'll whup us again."

"Then *you* tell 'im."

"Criminy. All *right!*" Shuffling feet resumed a reluctant ascent.

I peered around the jamb of the waiting room door. Two boys stood on the third step down.

One lad said diffidently, "You the doc?"

"I am."

"Ma said we had ter come on here."

I stepped aside and the boys filed past. I chuckled. Twins they were not, except that each sported a left eye puffy with the promise of a shiner, and each cradled a swollen right hand in its mate.

I reassured myself that neither boy's eye was damaged, that bruised lids would be tomorrow's badge of honor. No x-rays were needed to diagnose identical hand injuries, classical boxer's fractures of the fifth-finger metacarpal.

I said to the older boy, "You are?"

"Tom Anderson."

"Anson's boy?"

"He's my pa."

I turned to the younger boy. "And you are?"

"Ted, and he's my pa, too."

"How did this happen?"

Tom glanced at Ted. "Hit . . . the wall. Accidental."

"And your eye? Did the wall strike back?"

"Maybe it was a door. Sure."

I said, "Swung back and popped you right in the eye, I'll bet."

Admiration dawned in Tom's good eye. "That's what done 'er."

Ted said in his boy soprano, "That door has *got* to go."

I guided the boys into my treatment room. "Now I have to straighten those broken bones."

Ted backed away. "Ay, not me."

"Do you want to go through life with your little finger pointing south like that?"

"Don't care."

I sighed. "What would your ma say?"

Tom said, "Criminy."

Road to Trouble

SOMETIMES IT IS BETTER to be lucky than to be smart. That aphorism holds especially true when one leaves "smart" at home. The shortest way to Chippewa Lake was a fifty-five mile jaunt on Minnesota State Highway 65 through the central part of sprawling Koochiching County. The road led through a certifiable wilderness, finally edging close to the reservation. It was the most casually maintained state highway in Minnesota: a dirt track a lane and a half wide, in the good parts. Mostly I enjoyed the trip, with its forests and the wild creatures otherwise seen only in a zoo. There were adventures, though.

One day Barbara and I had just crossed the meandering Little Fork River when we met Butch Terrence coming down the broad bank the stream had carved during its youth. He drove a Mack tractor and pulled a trailer loaded with pulpwood cut into eight-foot lengths. Fresh snow covered the road, some six inches—worth. The usual practice when meeting a loaded truck was for me to pull off as far as I could, allowing the truck to inch past. I did my part, snuggling up against the snow bank, and waited.

Butch was in a hurry that day and didn't want to lose momentum approaching an odd thirty-degree up-ramp onto the bridge I had just crossed. He jake-braked, a little. Just before he reached the spot where Barbara and I waited in our Ford, his right-side wheels slid into the ditch. I saw him jerk the steering wheel, but Highway 65 won.

There is something about the sight of eight cords of pulpwood flying off their trailer, headed straight for a car that suddenly seems as much protection as an empty tin can, that makes you hope you haven't missed a payment on your life insurance. The logs landed with a magnificent whomp two feet from my door. Butch's tractor ended up opposite me as I stared across the abrupt log pile into its cab. I will never forget the wild expression on the man's face as he held onto that useless steering wheel with knuckles squeezed white. His truck cab had been totaled, twisted the way one wrings out a towel.

Our most harrowing adventure on old 65 came on a day when we arrived at Chippewa Lake after tunneling through swirling, light snow. By the time we left for home, conditions had degenerated into a blizzard. We skidded through snow piling higher by the minute and left the deep woods to turn north, still some twelve miles from Northpine. I accelerated smoothly in high gear when suddenly . . .

A drift two to three feet deep appeared on the road in front of us. We plowed into it before I had time to downshift. Fishtailing and sluing, we almost made it through the hundred-foot-long bank. Compacted snow jerked the steering wheel from my grasp and the old Ford skidded grill-first into the ditch. The car was at right angles to the road, back wheels on the snowy shoulder, front ones well down the bank.

I applied power to the rear wheels. They spun and we edged farther into the ditch. I had a snow scoop but had not thought to bring survival clothing. I shoveled. The car slid six inches deeper. I had never before confronted personal disaster.

Highway 65 was used primarily by loggers. In the gloom of a blizzardy night, with temperatures at twenty below zero and a snarling wind, the only certainty was that no one would happen along to help us. We were still five miles from the nearest farm, with terrain in between that was a clone of Antarctica's. We were on our own.

The only other implement in the trunk of the car was a bumper jack. Would it—?

When desperate, one does desperate things.

We jacked up the car by its rear bumper and then pushed it off the jack. An inch or two gained. Again. Twenty times again. The howling wind revealed glimpses of the moon when it blew clouds across its face. I was convinced it laughed at us. And again. Still again. Inch by painful inch, we regained the relative safety of the roadway. Another half hour of shoveling. We made it, caked in snow, too cold to feel cold.

We took this as an omen. Trade in lucky for a modicum of smart. From then on we traveled to Chippewa Lake by way of a paved, frequented highway, even though it extended the trip to seventy-five miles each way.

Oh, yes: we invested in a trunkful of survivor gear.

Arne

MY HOMETOWN OF NORTHPINE sits just south of good-neighbor Canada, from whence we get most of our weather. During summer months, a majority of the patients I saw each day were tourists. None of them left Minneapolis or Chicago with the intention of staying in our beautiful little hospital. Despite that, a generous number of them did. One memorable "visitor" was Arne Maki.

Arne suffered his heart attack while on a canoe trip. At the age of thirty-four, he was square as a cement block and twice as solid. City life had leached away conditioning, leaving weight-lifter muscles laced with fat.

Arne's chest pain began while he and his twelve-year-old son, Matte, were breaking camp one morning in July. They paddled through four lakes, a good dozen miles in all, and portaged three times, including over rugged Dead Man's Ridge, before they caught up with Terry Mark, a timber cruiser for the Minnesota and Ontario Paper Company. Terry brought them to Northpine Hospital.

Arne's face was gray, damp, and cold as a sponge left in the refrigerator. His EKG showed the electrical spoor of a huge myocardial infarction, a heart attack involving the left pumping chamber. His blood serum was so choked with fats and cholesterol that it settled into white layers like milk and cream.

I put him to bed, ordered oxygen and morphine, and found

a place for Matte to stay. We settled down to wait. Arne lived through the night. During the next two days he improved, and he was in a condition to talk by the third.

"That must have hurt," I said. He nodded. "Where all did you feel it?" He pointed to his chest, his jaw, down his left arm. I said, "I'm trying to imagine what it must have been like, miles into the wilderness and all that pain." He shrugged. "Matte says you carried the canoe over that hellacious portage."

"Matte couldn't heft it."

"Not ideal treatment for a heart attack." I mimed placing a hat over my heart. "My respect for your determination is enormous." His shoulders twitched again.

Arne spent three weeks as our guest. We shook hands the day he left. He looked at me solemnly, his round face as impassive as ever.

He said, "Thanks."

Almost a year later, I sat at the hospital nurses' desk doing chart work. A shadow fell across my sheets of paper. I glanced up.

A man square as a cement block and twice as solid studied me solemnly. My mind raced: a past patient, tourist—what was his name? Canoe trip. Heart attack—

He handed me a huge box of candy, then strode to the lobby and vanished. Maki! That was his name, Arne Maki.

Neither of us had said a word.

Pass Catcher

NORTHPINE HOSPITAL was a Cape Cod cottage sporting a bit of a sprawl, which gave it a homey ambience. In addition to hospital necessities, the two-story building made room for my office and a five-room apartment where we lived: Barbara, Mary and Bruce—the first two of our brood of six children—and I. Mostly such togetherness was handy, but it could lead to interesting dramas. Take the night Eleanor Jenson had her baby.

The layout of the apartment was such that the door from the hospital entered the kitchen. Next came the dining room, a living room, and two bedrooms. I was asleep that night when the bedside telephone rang. Now, I realize the instrument is inanimate, but I swear sometimes it conveys urgency despite the fact.

It sounded urgent.

I answered accordingly and nurse's aide Esther Phillips screamed into my ear, "An OB just came in. Complete. *Hurry!*"

I had thrown back the covers when Esther burst through the hospital doorway, dashed through the kitchen to the dining room, and made a sharp left. I met her in the brief hallway. "She's bulging. Elsie [the other nurse] says come STAT!" (Esther was a recent student of medical terminology and liked to throw around her newly acquired verbiage.) I passed Miss Phillips in the dining room.

Maybe I should back up a bit. In those halcyon days, I slept in the nude. In the confusion of the moment, I was already to the kitchen in my, uh, natural state. Miss Phillips screeched again, but not an OB-About-to-Deliver screech this time, more of an Emperor's-New-Clothes screech. There is a difference. I charged past Miss Phillips again. She did a pirouette that would have won her a spot in some ballet troupe. In the bedroom I found my undershorts. Back to the kitchen, where I spied my galoshes and jumped into them. They were there, why not? I galumphed down the short corridor to the delivery room just as Mrs. Jenson decided enough was enough, and she gave that special push known so well to mothers.

I went to my knees and caught baby girl Jenson two feet off the floor. She peed on my arm in thanks.

So there I was, kneeling in my red-and-white polka-dot undershorts and galoshes. By golly, if I had shown anywhere near as much pass-catching skill while I played for the Winona State College football warriors, I might have earned a letter.

One never knows when some arcane skill will save the day.

Little Herbie

ONE SUNDAY AFTERNOON I received a terse telephone call from nurse Joan Adams: "Child run over by a car."

I ran the two hundred feet separating my new home from the back door of the hospital.

Herbie sat on the emergency room table, bellowing in the key of C-flat minor. His disposition took a turn for the worse when he spied me. (I wonder if people know how disconcerting it is to meet a mother and child in Meinert's Market and have the youngster throw a fit upon seeing you.) Herbie's mother Angela hovered in the background. She was one of those fluttery women—hair, hands, blinking eyelids. I recognized the man with her to be John Ellingson, a logger with a contract out in Dentaybo Township. Sweat poured down his broad Scandinavian face.

"Doc," he said, "that kid darted out in front of me. I pulled to the right to miss him, but darned if he didn't reverse his field. He rolled under my car like one them tumbleweeds you read about."

I sent John to the waiting room, where coffee's gift of rejuvenation awaited. Then I set out to examine Herbie.

Now, someone six feet tall and weighing 175 pounds can easily cope physically with a three-year-old child.

Maybe not.

I turned to his mother. "Perhaps you could help me calm him down."

"Oh, I never discipline Herbie," she said earnestly. "It interferes with development of a strong ego."

I trust that I hid my thoughts: this lad needs no more vitamins for his ego. I did what I had learned worked best under such circumstances: I sent Angela on a search for the equivalent of a left-handed monkey wrench, then had no-nonsense nurse (and experienced grandma) Joan Adams restrain Herbie's ego long enough for me to assess the damage.

I added up the score.

Herbie:

    Abrasions: Seven, all minor.

    Lacerations: Two, one requiring a small tape to close it.

    Bruises: Three or four and counting.

    Broken bones: None.

    Serious injuries: None.

John Ellingson's new car:

    Tires: Two month's wear removed in three seconds.

    Body: A crumpled front fender from meeting up with a village lamppost, which now canted at a rakish fifteen degrees.

I reassured John and called Angela back into the emergency room.

I said, "I'm happy to report that Herbie shows no sign of serious injury. I may be speaking out of turn to say this, but your son regularly causes traffic hazards. He constantly plays in the middle of the street and sometimes he refuses to get out of the way. Why, just last week I had to stop for him myself. I wonder if you shouldn't do something about that."

Angela gazed at me with her habitual expression of bewilderment.

"But Doctor, I *always* dress him in red!"

Emil

NORTHPINE HOSPITAL was the last building in town. Forests stretched for miles north and east of it, second-growth timber large enough to interest local loggers. Our backyard ended in the same tangle of trees. One night at 3:00 A.M. I trudged toward the hospital, more asleep than not. A bobcat screeched from thirty feet away and I'm certain my feet left the ground. The cry of a wildcat drags claws across the blackboard of one's soul. Magnify the sound of ten alley cats in a brawl: it falls short.

The creature squalled again. I ran for the hospital, for I knew primal fear, the unacknowledged core emotion of our species. I responded to the most feral sound I had ever heard.

The most feral, that is, until the day I received a call from Emil Gruber's farm.

Northpine had a large German population, many of whom had immigrated just after World War II. For them, Deutsch remained the preferred tongue. I spoke a modicum of the language.

As for Emil Gruber, I was never quite sure if he understood me, or I him, but our problem arose from more than language. Emil's friend, Wayne Baade, sometimes brought him to the office. One day I told Wayne of my frustrations. He rolled his eyes and said, "*Ich versteh*. That's just Emil."

Sometimes Emil passed out in a public place, during mass,

at Meinert's Market, at a Saturday evening whist party. I attended him for several of these episodes. They followed a pattern: collapse and spasm; return to awareness soon after Father Julian administered last rites. Like a good soldier, Emil would lie flat on his back at dress attention. Periodically he exploded into odd muscular twitching that fit no syndrome known to neurology, not drug- or alcohol-induced, not a true seizure disorder. His tightly closed eyelids resisted all attempts to open them. When he awoke, it was always with, *"Guten Tag, Herr Doktor. Was* do you here?"

Brunhilda Wasserberger was his sister. She hovered over Emil, to the eternal distraction of her husband, Werner. For me, the sequence of events would be a call from church, or the Hot Spot Café, or the Liebschs', where the whist party was nicely started—"Send *schnell* the *Krankenwagen*"—and the ambulance would return with Emil at about the same time Brunhilda arrived with Father Julian in tow. "The rites, Father, oh *bitte*. He'll die without the rites!"

Four times in my presence Emil Gruber received the sacrament. He always walked away none the worse for it.

One day in May, Brunhilda called me at the office. "He's dead, Dr. MacDonald. *Mach quick schnell.* And bring Father Julian." I grabbed my medical satchel and told nurse Elaine to call the priest. "I'll be right back; it's only Emil."

The man lived fifteen miles out, in New Bavaria Township. As I drove, I stewed over my precious schedule, waiting patients. Would he be awake when I got there? He usually timed his resurrections with my appearance, or that of Father Julian. It was always a temptation not to go, but that nag—old "Dr. What If?"—would grab me by the ear. This time, RAM, what if?

I first heard the sound while I was still a quarter of a mile from

Emil's place. A squalling out of Dante's nightmare throbbed, directionless. Twenty cars lined the driveway. I charged into Emil's house, but a commotion out back dragged me through the empty building into the barnyard. Here were a dozen solemn men, one armed with a deer rifle.

The sound was now a thunder that twisted my guts. Tethered to the back of a truck was a great Swiss bull, bellowing rhythmically. Hands clasped in frantic prayer, Brunhilda stood to one side. She shrieked and ran at me.

"*Ach, Herr Doktor, Gott sei dank,* you're here. *Wo ist* Father Julian?" I winced at the uproar and asked where. She pointed. "Terrible. Out there."

"Out there" proved to be a pasture beyond the barn. As a farmer, Emil dreamed beyond his willingness to maintain. His pasture was a dense thicket of one-inch poplar trees, vagrant sprouts allowed to grow. I spied a knot of men through the brush; they looked everywhere but toward the center of the circle they formed. They opened their ranks for me.

"My God," I said. I dropped to my knees beside what was left of Emil. "How?"

"The bull," someone said. I rolled Emil's body onto its back and listened with my stethoscope, an inane gesture before such devastation. We doctors are captives of rote.

Emil's friend Wayne explained what had happened. "Near as we can tell, Doc, Emil came in here with his bull. He'd raised that animal from a calf and wouldn't even ring its nose. 'Gentle,' he'd always say, 'that bull's my friend.' We all tried to tell him, 'don't believe it.'"

Suddenly I saw a pattern, a serpentine maze of broken saplings, winding about the pasture. Homer Gast said, "That devil would stomp him for a while, then butt him farther through the brush. I called Wayne and Karl. We got ropes on him. Scared us, him so wild, but we had to. At first we didn't know for sure about Emil—" Abruptly he turned his back, swiped at his eyes with a calloused hand. "Then we was sure."

Father Julian trotted toward us, his lips as pale as his eyes, all whites. He knelt and gave Emil his final last rites.

During all the time we attended to Emil, the bull continued to roar, a relentless, frenzied beat. The creature stood with legs widespread, yanking at ropes that bound him to the truck. Foam lathered his flanks and chest, and his eyes rolled wildly at anyone who came within his view. His maw gaped with each bellow. The sound pounded, harmonics that clutched breath. In all my life I have heard nothing to rival that thunder of rage and bloodlust.

Wayne Baade strode to Sid Donner, the man with the rifle. "Give me the gun." There were tear tracks in the mud on Wayne's face. He strode to within ten feet of the bull.

"Devil!" He raised the rifle. The creature thrashed at its ropes and the truck moved grudgingly. "Die slow!" The animal's eyes bulged and he roared his challenge. Wayne fired. A rose blossomed on the broad chest of the bull. It jerked, and one rope broke. Wayne fired again and a second red stain appeared on the bull's tawny side. The animal dropped to its knees.

A third shot. The bull tried to roar but coughed blood that splattered the truck. A fourth rifle crack. The beast sprawled onto its side and convulsed. Wayne went to stand by its nose. He held the muzzle against its broad forehead and pulled the trigger one last time.

The Great Train Ride

I HAVE HEARD THE ARGUMENTS against house calls—lack of resources, inconvenience, inefficiency—and, like most rationalizations, they hold a kernel of truth mixed with a fistful of wishful thinking. To my notion, the advantages of seeing for myself what conditions my patients lived in offset most of the disadvantages.

"House call"—the simple phrase makes even that adventure sound mundane. They were not always. I have traveled to a swamp shack riding on the rear end of a tractor through water up to its hubcaps to see Grandma in her natural setting. And there was the time George drove me across a frozen lake into Canada to see his mother. I had no license to practice medicine in Ontario, a minor detail when need makes rules inane. So far I have not been summoned to Ottawa to explain.

A rail line ran through Northpine, a single track starting in St. Paul and petering out somewhere north of here. I'm not sure why; maybe Canada got in the way. This particular night, the telephone rang and I was half-asleep when I answered. It was Dodd Johnson, one of the track-maintenance men. He said I had a patient out in Wildwood. I mumbled something appropriate, like "Where's that?" He vowed to show me and said to meet him at the railroad depot and to "dress real warm, Doc."

When this great country was first ravaged (well, *developed*), the railroad was king of transportation. Tracks were laid on the whims of a gaggle of civil engineers. When roads were built, they tended to follow existing rail lines. Wildwood was an anomaly. Fifteen miles south of Northpine, for reasons long forgotten, the highway wandered well away from its forebear. An old railroad-watering and firewood-fueling station still existed, an anachronism in the remotest part of this bypassed bight of track.

Every fall some of the Really Important People associated with the railroad came to Wildwood in a tastefully decorated private rail car to participate in the gentlemanly avocation of shooting deer. The daily train deposited the dignified assemblage and its hotel-on-wheels on a siding at Wildwood. C. Randall Jameson was the leader of this merry band of sportsmen. We know at once that he is not your everyday VIP: truly important VIPs are addressed as Initial-Name-Name. After his first day of hunting, plowing through terrain certifiably wild, C. Randall's heart sustained an infarction: he had a heart attack. This event left him with a small problem because the locomotive employed by his railroad company passed this lonely stretch of track only twice a day, at 6:00 A.M. going north and 8:00 P.M. headed south. Dodd Johnson had been summoned by the magic of telegraphy.

I arrived at the depot to find Dodd waiting for me on an open-air speeder. We were enjoying a mid-November cold snap, translatable as twenty-five degrees below zero. So there we were, on that speeder, ready to go. Now, fifteen miles doesn't sound so far, provided one has reasonable modes of transportation— such as crawling, walking, even driving—but on a speeder with no top, on a night I was willing to call cold, it becomes to-the-moon-and-back lengthy. It quickly became apparent to me, huddled there on the floor of that thingamajig, that one, the windshield is misnamed—its real purpose is to funnel arctic air down onto anyone naïve enough to sit with his back against it; two, there is no ideal speed: slow impossibly prolongs the cold and fast is worse; three, icy air can induce asthma in a non-asthmatic doctor; and four, there is no disgrace in being carried bodily into a private car by two burly railroad employees.

How did things turn out? Quite well. Within half an hour I was toasty warm. Once my frozen fingers thawed enough to prepare a shot of morphine, C. Randall too improved.

We waited together, chatting, getting acquainted. (I'm not certain that C. Randall considered our visit the high point of his trip.) His train was only two hours late when it hooked onto our car. Did you notice the possessive pronoun? How quickly we plebeians acquire a taste for luxury.

Back at Northpine, I offered C. Randall the accommodations of our fine little hospital. He refused. I waxed eloquent, explaining the limitations of even so grand a railroad car as his. He demurred. What I learned from our exchange was that commoners babble while those in charge just say no.

C. Randall's locomotive took him back south that evening, destination St. Paul. I'm not much of a mystic—I don't see hidden meaning in ordinary events—but it did occur to me that St. Paul was probably a better destination than that other beloved community in southern Minnesota, St. Peter.

Grit

GOD, FATE, NATURE—take your choice—grant a rural family physician the opportunity to see human beings at their very best. Quiet courage: not the kind that earns medals, the kind that sustains.

Julia Franklin taught piano. She gracefully carried the physique of a Wagnerian soprano, and while she was every inch and pound a *grand dame,* she had no arrogance about her. Music was her passion, one she inspired in her students, even those of modest talent. How she arrived from Boston at as unlikely a place as Northpine I never learned.

I met Julia when she asked me to stop by and see her husband at home. I knocked on her door that snowy day, my shiny new medical grip in hand. She smiled at me, a regal salute, and led me into the living room.

Elias Franklin lay on the sofa. I sized him up quickly: flushed, sweating, eyes wide circles in a face lean and anxious. He raised a hand in greeting. Its motion was jerky and uncoordinated. A wasted foot protruded from under a blanket; it began to kick in a crescendo of clonic spasms. Elias Franklin seized his thigh in both hands until the thumping foot subsided.

"Hello, Doctor," Elias coughed weakly. "Thanks for coming." He struggled to clear his throat of mucus. It came out pink.

Julia Franklin said, "Elias has been like this since last evening." She tucked a stray lock of hair into a swirl coiled on her head. "The cough and fever. He has been bedridden with multiple sclerosis for more than fifteen years."

I opened my grip and hauled out my tools. I heard rales at the base of his right lung, crepitant whispers made by air bubbling through fluid. Elias Franklin had pneumonia. When I told them I planned to move him to the hospital, Julia asked, "Can you treat him here?" I halted my professional bustle and explained the need for an x-ray.

She said, "I trust your diagnostic skills."

"Nursing care," I bleated.

She drew herself fiercely erect. "We have managed all this time."

"I guess I could give him shots of penicillin here." I prepared a dose from the miniature pharmacy I carried so proudly in my grip. Afterward I said, "I've been reading about a new idea in treating multiple sclerosis using prostigmine shots, a kind of chemical stimulant. Would you be interested in trying this?"

For the first time Julia's control cracked, and I saw in her eyes what a decade and a half of continuous care had done. She recovered quickly.

Elias said, "What have I to lose?"

I said, "Then I'll order some. In the meantime, I'll stop by each day to give you penicillin."

MS, that scourge of vibrant youth, vanquishes hope and destroys sturdy bodies implacably. Even today no cure exists. In 1950 crackpot schemes and fads abounded, even within the ranks of sincere physicians. I had little faith in my proposed treatment.

The prostigmine experiment lasted about six months. On Wednesday afternoons I stopped at the Franklins for an injection of hope, a visit, a cup of tea, and one of Julia's cookies. We discussed life and music and the trials of teaching. Occasionally Julia played for me, Chopin or Debussy. I missed our visits after lack of improvement in Elias's condition made it clear the Franklins could find better use for their scant funds.

During the following months, I saw Elias occasionally: pressure sores, urinary-tract infections—the bane of MS patients. It was in March of 1953 that I was called to attend Julia.

An ambulance brought her to the hospital. She lay propped up in bed, pasty as a bank of snow, clammy and as cold in her own sweat. Her eyelids flickered at the sound of my voice. "It hurts, Doctor," she said, her words swallowed in a hissing oxygen mask. "My chest."

Fluid crackled in her lungs and an electrical heart tracing, an EKG, showed massive damage to her left pumping chamber. Julia Franklin was mortally wounded.

The day crept along and Julia was still with us. Her blood pressure was less than the touch of her bed sheets. Her hands and feet existed without appreciable circulation. The death smell of a huge heart attack permeated her room. I visited her hourly and spent the night in the doctors' lounge. The fierce old lady snorted and gurgled, and her color remained ghastly, her blood pressure resistant to attempts to prod it by chemistry. In the morning I returned to her bedside, tired and unshaven. She muttered in her stupor, a soft rumble under the mask. There was a pattern to the sounds. I lifted the mask for a moment and put my ear near her lips.

"I must not die," she whispered, "I must not . . ."

I replaced the mask and dampened a cloth to soothe her forehead. A tear ran down my cheek.

.   .   .

Julia Franklin went home twenty days later. Her daughter left for Boston after staying an extra week. Julia took her pills faithfully—her digitalis heart stimulant, diuretics to keep fluid from collecting. She resumed her teaching duties.

Julia called me to the house one day. Elias had not awakened that morning. He lay stuporous in his bed, his temperature 105 degrees. She made no objection when I called for an ambulance to take him to the hospital. He lingered for three days with overwhelming sepsis from another urinary-tract infection. His was a peaceful death. My old friend drew a deep breath at 6:10 A.M. and never followed it up with another.

After I had signed the forms that "made it official," I drove to their small house and roused Julia. She crawled back into bed, propped on a mound of pillows. I told her how sorry I was and assured her that he had not suffered. I stood next to the bed, ready to support her in her grief. She looked out the window, then back at me. She smiled. If I had to choose a phrase to describe her aspect, I'd have said "at peace." She said, "Thank you, Doctor, you've been good to us."

Julia Franklin remained a faithful patient, taking her medications as I had prescribed them. I counted those that remained to make sure. The community honored her at her funeral, which came eight days after Elias's.

The State of Minnesota expected me to name a cause of death. The bureaucrat in charge of such matters balked at my entry. I had scrawled, "No longer refused to die."

Fishing

M INNESOTA PROPAGANDA MILLS give wide credence to
the notion that people occasionally catch fish out of our
famed lakes and streams. In no Chamber of Commerce blurbs
have I seen it acknowledged that the reverse occurs. I stand to
speak for Pisces!

For years we kept a trophy board in the emergency room of
Northpine Hospital to acknowledge Fish Who Caught People:
hooks I had removed from sundry parts of human anatomy. We
stuck them into the green felt covering a cutout of a large, leer-
ing fish and labeled them with the name of the donor. It elicited
much favorable comment.

Agnes Herrmann ("two *r*s, two *n*s, Doc.") was jolly and round.
I once heard a psychiatrist insist that fat people only appear to
be jolly and are really burning inside with suppressed aggres-
sions which they cope with poorly and cover up with a façade of
cheeriness, but Agnes *was* jolly and wasn't consumed with anger
at all, except on one occasion, which I am about to recount, and
she wasn't suppressing a single iota of anger then. Unfortunately, fat people have more than their share of medical problems, no matter how merry they might be. I knew Agnes well.

Agnes did everything she could from a sit-down position.
This included fishing. She lived year-round in a nice little house
on Long Lake. It was, well, comfortable, maybe not completely

clean—rather the way one would envision the home of a person who was jolly and happy and did things from a sit-down position.

A rickety dock leaned into the lake in front of her house. Every nice evening she moved her extra-wide lawn chair to the end of the dock. She knew the depth of the water out as far as she could cast. She put a bobber on her line at the precise point needed to send her bait minnow scurrying about just off the bottom. From then on, fishing consisted of leaning back with a comfortable sigh, gazing down the lake toward the sunset, monitoring the neighbors: those back for the summer, who was barbecuing supper outdoors, which party had company while the missus was off in Minneapolis—that sort of thing. She kept track of what her bobber was up to. Two or three times an evening it would do a hula in the calm water, plop under, and she had her breakfast.

One evening Agnes Herrmann sat in her usual place. A boat appeared from the west, a fourteen-foot Lund aluminum with "Long Lake Resort" stenciled on its bow. A City Feller sat in the stern; she knew he was City by the way he zigzagged every time he cast out. He had a plug big enough for a kid to use as a toy boat.

Closer he came, flinging that plug toward shore. City came abreast of Agnes. She waved at him, neighborly, but he didn't respond. Once more he zinged it out and it rattled on the dock behind her. He yanked and, as Agnes described it, "It was like a danged eagle landing on my arm! All its claws sank in.... That City, he jerked and straightened out the line. I let out a screech you could hear in Hong Kong. City cut his line and took off down the lake, tight as he could go. Dang it, Doc, a cast and run!"

Physician, Heal Thyself. Please!

DOCTORS make the worst patients in the world. Physicians wryly regard this statement as an aphorism. I've known nurses to agree with an unbecoming enthusiasm. Perhaps it has something to do with the time-honored relationship between the two professions: doctors speak, nurses respond meekly and jump to obey. I have intimations that this fine hierarchical arrangement is crumbling. Is nothing sacred?

Over the years I have had a few of my colleagues as patients. The problem arises, of course, in deciding which doctor is in charge. Doctors are control addicts. To surrender power to another, even a colleague, violates some fine-print tenet of the Hippocratic oath. All right, *mea culpa.*

Dr. F. Caldwell Kleinmutter came north to get away from it all. He bestowed his patronage on Johnson's Rustic Inn Resort, the famous northern hideaway. Dr. Kleinmutter was an eminent surgeon who held court in a renowned medical factory. People came from far away so he could rearrange their parts. All the while, lower-case colleagues clustered at his elbow. I knew of Dr. Kleinmutter, which didn't distinguish me in particular because so did readers of the *Minneapolis Tribune* and *Time* magazine. Destiny winked at me, and I became Dr. Kleinmutter's personal physician.

A Sunday afternoon, the Minnesota Twins on TV. I trudged

along a corridor leading to the hospital emergency room. *Again.*
Halfway down the hall, I became aware of an uproar. A sputtering masculine voice launched winged words I had not heard in such profusion since my last night in an army barracks.

Three citizens occupied the emergency room. In a corner stood Greg Johnson, the dignified patriarch of the family corporation running Johnson's Resort. Nurse Edna Freeman stood beside the examination table. The grin on her face broke through all efforts to preserve a façade of professional calm. The man lying on the table waved energetically in rough coincidence with his rumbling monologue, not an easy task when one is stretched out prone.

Edna said, "This is Dr. Kleinmutter."

The name failed to register with me, in the same sense that one introduced to God, not really believing, might ask, "God who?" I went to the head of the table and asked, "Sir, what seems to be the problem?"

Dr. Kleinmutter roared, "Problem! Are you blind?"

Edna whipped off the sheet covering my colleague with a flourish that would have done credit to a matador. The man was of sturdy build. A broad expanse of Eddie Bauer twill representing the seat of his trousers was festooned with fishing lures. Rapalas and Bass-masters, dare-devils of three hues, single hooks and gangs, plastic worms, Mepps, bucktail-spinners—the man's britches looked like a bait-store rummage sale. I touched a three-hook golden Rapala plug.

Dr. Kleinmutter hollered, "Ouch, damn it! Don't *wiggle* those things."

I said, "They seem to be hooked into your—into you."

"Brilliant!"

"How—?"

"I was victim of a pusillanimous attack."

I nearly giggled and hysteria threatened. Fish lures at twenty paces! Don't turn your back! I stifled it. Barely. A fish with a sense of humor? Maybe a sturgeon, of honored and ancient pedigree.

Dr. Kleinmutter said, "The thug who claimed to be a guide did this."

Greg Johnson said mildly, "You were still-fishing in an anchored boat."

"Allowed this to happen. A huge wave made me lose my balance and I slid backwards off my seat. That miscreant of a guide distracted me and I had neglected to close my tackle box."

I piped up, "You carry a large inventory of baits."

He said, "Bent my tackle box all to—Look, do you intend to do something about this mess?"

I glanced at the outpatient chart. There it was, written boldly as gospel: F. Caldwell Kleinmutter, M.D., Ph.D., F.A.C.S—the whole schmeer.

I stuttered, "Sir, the first decision—Uh, you aren't *the* Dr. Klein—Oh my. What are you doing way up here?"

"What decision, what, what?"

"Your pants. We can't slide them down, pegged in place like that, and I can't see well enough to free these lures. . . . Do you realize you have twenty-seven hooks—"

"Goddamn."

"First I'll have to cut off your trousers. They'll be in shreds, you understand."

"Goddamn. Ouch! God*damn!*"

Hospital custodian Art Carlson went shopping at the Federated Store for new pants. Dr. Kleinmutter donated all twenty-seven hooks to our Fish-Who-Caught-People trophy board, and Shad Zeitung from the newspaper showed up with his camera to take F. Caldwell's picture for *County Weekly*. Seems Art had bumped into Shad downtown. News travels fast around here.

Dr. Kleinmutter and I parted friends. He promised to write, but so far he hasn't.

Feud

I STRODE BRISKLY toward Room Three of my office, experiencing my usual tingle of anticipation. What problem awaits, oh Medical Fates? I glanced at the name on the fresh, new chart I picked up from beside the door. Bartholomew Vargas. Even dressed in casual clothing, the man radiated Quality.

"What brings you here today?" I asked.

His eyes gave up "worried" long enough to inspect me briefly. "Chest pain," he said. "It began last evening. I know I should have come then."

"Tell me more about it."

He patted a broad, muscular chest to the left of his sternum. "Here. Stabbing sensations, an ache, and ... I don't know how to describe it ... a restless feeling, one of impending doom." He shook his head. "How difficult it is to describe a sensation."

I asked my questions: his age (fifty-two), problems with breathing or pain radiating down his arm or to his jaw, previous discomfort during exertion—the usual gamut. I examined him, collecting a pageful of "normal"s as I moved through the systems of the body, including lungs clear as a spring day and a heart performing with strength and authority. I ordered a chest x-ray, blood tests, and an electrical tracing, an EKG, of his heart.

"Your cardiogram is normal," I said, reporting back to Mr. Vargas, "which brings me to another issue." I pondered, as always, how to broach the topic of symptoms produced by twinges in the psyche. Most people view a diagnosis of psychosomatic distress as a personal attack, a vote of no confidence in their ability to cope. I prayed for inspiration. "Has there been any unusual event in your life recently?"

Bartholomew Vargas sighed, a deep sound. "Doctor, may I see that EKG?"

I started. "The actual tracing? Well, yes." I handed him the six-foot-long piece of paper ribbon. He began at the proper end and flipped it along in a most professional manner. My scalp tingled as I considered implications. "You can read these? Sir?"

He smiled abruptly and extended a hand. "Forgive me, I should have introduced myself more completely. I'm Dr. Bartholomew Vargas, head of the Department of Internal Medicine at Great Southern University." He shifted his gaze to a spot over my shoulder. "I'm struggling with an uncomfortable fact." His eyes were pleading when they sought mine again. "I've never considered myself a—a twitch. But there it is. I came north to—to get as far away as I could. You understand."

"Well . . ."

He said briskly, "You have heard of Dr. Montgomery Sears?"

"He was a guest lecturer while I was in medical school."

"And Dr. Gamble Ward?"

"Of course! They're both at Great Southern University."

"Perhaps you have also heard of the bloody feud that rages between these two, uh, brilliant men?"

"Oh, yes, one of our surgery profs in medical school regaled us—Uh, yes, I have."

"Genius at work and head-on in conflict." He sighed again, and I was reminded of wind blowing through a lonesome pine. "I was ordered by the administration of the university to forge a truce between these, uh, gentlemen. I left them the day before yesterday."

Good Fudge Requires
the Best Ingredients

E D WAS MY INTERNSHIP ROOMMATE. When I think of
him, I think of the time we made fudge, a requiem he
would have enjoyed.

An internship in 1947 was a period of forced servitude,
when salaries were miniscule and duties endless. Hospitals
balanced precarious budgets courtesy of such cheap labor. Doctors Grayhair and Oldtimer justified thirty-six-hour tours of
duty on the grounds that "by God, we had to, and so shall they.
Toughens 'em up." Bad ideas survive like crabgrass. Even today
the indentured slavery known as "the internship" persists in all
its archaic penuriousness and abuse.

This particular week we had drawn the night shift on obstetrics. As was typical of the capricious nature of that service,
we ran from one delivery room to the next until, suddenly, there
were no more mothers-in-waiting. It was 3:00 A.M. I looked at
Ed; he nodded.

The newborn nursery was adjacent to the obstetrical suite.
By tacit, even unplanned, agreement, we interns and collabo-
rating nurses kept a supply of nutritious food in the cramped
preparation room of the nursery: cream, cocoa, sugar, vanilla,
chopped nuts. There was a hot plate for important functions
like, oh, making fudge.

We measured and stirred and cooked. The candy was superb, melt-in-your-mouth tasty. Ed and I toasted each other in rich chocolate.

Sally Turner was the nurse on duty that night. She bustled into the prep room, her feet twinkling along in a way that made her seem always on tippy-toe. She opened the refrigerator and let out a subdued scream.

"What ho, Sally?" Ed said.

She waved her arms about like a Boy Scout practicing semaphore signaling. Her voice was almost strident. "The milk. Where did it go?"

A twinge tickled me between the shoulder blades. "What, uh, was the source of the milk in question?"

"Breast pump, mother's milk. What am I going to feed the premature babies?"

I held out the plate. "Sally, have a piece of fudge."

Home Delivery

I PICKED UP THE TELEPHONE. A voice said, "This is Cedric Crawford. My wife is in labor and we want you to come on out. Peaceful Valley Road."

I searched my internal map. "Which is where?"

"East of Trillium."

"Sir, who is your regular doctor?"

"You are."

Now the internal search was through my list of expectant mothers. "I don't recall a Crawford."

"She's never seen you before. When will you get here?"

"Labor, you said. When is she due? Any prenatal care? Home delivery? Holy buckets. Exactly where?"

Cedric Crawford considered. "It's complicated, how to get here, Doc. I'll wait in front of your office in Trillium."

Barbara and I sped toward the far southwestern corner of our vast county. As promised, Cedric Crawford sat on a bench in front of the hotel that housed my office. He resembled someone who had been hooked up to one of those static electricity machines: no two hairs adorning his face or head seemed content to associate with any two others. When he crawled into the backseat, I said, "We'll just follow your car."

"Don't got one. Better hurry."

"How far?"

"Hard to tell, walking and hitching. Maybe five miles."

· · ·

Cedric Crawford stopped me with a tap on the shoulder. "Here, Doc." I looked around. On the left, cedars and tamaracks and black spruce trees, on the right—

"Where's your house?"

Cedric Crawford jumped the ditch, a channel three feet deep carrying some twenty inches of water. He pointed along a footpath leading toward a confusion of cedars and tamaracks and black spruce.

My Barbara said, "I won't! My uniform, my shoes—I just won't."

I forded the small stream with her in my arms, she stiff as a department-store manikin. The path where Cedric stood jiggling impatiently dipped down, disappearing beneath brown swamp water. Our guide plowed into it noisily. "A little damp since that last rain," he said.

"Wait," I screeched. "How far?"

"Forty rods."

"Holy buckets."

Barbara said, "*I won't!*"

Cedric carried my supplies and I hoisted Barbara piggyback. I slogged in his wake. It is the nature of new love that touching and caressing, even carrying one's beloved about seem joyful. Barbara was a slip of a girl—well, perhaps *slip* isn't quite the right word. Sturdy. Those Swedish and Native American genes that were her heritage. I gave out at thirty rods and she slid feetfirst into the water. "It's that or both of us flat," I explained. She declined Cedric's offer to pinch-hit.

The cabin stood on a knoll. Swamp water lurked on all sides. My first impression was of constant motion: five boisterous tots, chickens fluttering before us like the bow wave of a ship, three hysterical dogs, and, of course, the mosquitoes. Didn't I mention them? It was impossible to breathe without inhaling a few. When one is carrying one's bride, reluctant passenger, through two feet of swamp water, hot and sweaty, a beacon to mosquitoes clear over on the next forty, there is little opportunity for evasive tactics and no time to swat.

The hut was of weathered logs. Grass adorned its top like a green butch haircut. Along with a chicken or two, children and dogs streamed into the cabin. I ordered Cedric to clear the place of small creatures, bipedal, four-footed, or feathered.

A woman lay on a homemade bed in one corner. She watched us anxiously for a moment, then moaned. I lifted the blanket covering her.

"Oh God! Quick, Barbara, open the pack—gloves—no time—"

A length of umbilical cord hung from the woman's vagina. "Push, lady!" I said. The baby's head was near the outlet of the birth canal. "You have a chance. Push!"

The child's head emerged, its body, chubby legs, and feet. Baby Crawford raised her arms in a startle response. Alive! She began to squall. "Cry, little lady," I said.

I put the baby in her mother's arms. "I don't even know your name."

"Katie," she said, "and this one's Jessie." She put a finger in Jessie's mouth and the babe tried to suck. Katie bared her breast. Jessie nuzzled for a moment and then went to sleep.

We packed our things. Cedric sat down beside Katie and took her hand. "We are lucky," he said.

"Lucky indeed," I said, "a prolapsed umbilical cord. It must have happened just as we arrived."

"I don't know about all that. I meant *lucky*. Look at all them fine children."

I said, "A man can be proud."

As we headed back to our car, Barbara plowed through water with the abandon of a child playing in puddles. I splashed to keep up. "I'm sorry, had no idea. Your uniform is a total mess."

"You can buy me a new one."

I shut her car door and squished to the other side. I pulled off my shoes and poured swamp water onto the road. "I baptize you in the name of Jessie Crawford," I said. Turning to Barbara, I asked, "How can I make this up to you?"

"You can't." She glanced at me and smiled, her patented explosion kind. "But you can try. You have mud all over your face." When she rubbed my cheek with a handkerchief, I took her hand and pulled her toward me, and for a while the mosquitoes didn't seem quite as bad.

Henry and Lily

IT IS COMMON KNOWLEDGE that country doctors sometimes received payment in unorthodox currencies and in touchingly earnest ways. I delivered a son for the wife of Native American Conroy Makwa. He sent me an envelope containing fifty cents every month or two. I finally had to tell him to quit when he had paid my obstetrical fee of $35.00. Other people from Chippewa Lake Reservation paid me with large bags of wild rice so often that my kids grew up thinking potatoes were a special treat.

Beyond "payment," there at "pioneer" mid-twentieth century, hospitality was traditional and sincere.

Henry and Lily Zilliox farmed three forties west of Trillium. Trees hemmed in their fields like frowning kibitzers. They lived in a sturdy north woods house, plain but clean, with floors of scrubbed bare boards.

Henry had come to see me on my first day in Trillium. The man was pale as a snow bank. His hemoglobin tested out at 4.6 grams, about thirty percent of what it should have been. Those red cells he did have were huge ones typical of pernicious anemia. Over the following weeks, his hemoglobin climbed steadily under a magical prod from shots of liver extract. He and Lily were inordinately impressed. I confess to a dash of smugness, and I almost felt a cheat with my insider awareness of what the injections would do.

One day in mid-September when the Zillioxes came to the office, Lily said to Barbara, "We'd like to have you and Doctor come to our place for lunch on Thursday." Our next visit to Trillium loomed as a special event.

The Zillioxes had four sons. Two were married and lived in side-by-side houses across the road, while the two bachelors still lived in the family home. All worked the farm together.

The day featured September at its most winsome. Warm breezes rustled leaves painted scarlet and yellow or oak-tree russet. Nature sang of the joys of sloth.

The Zillioxes were waiting for us. When we drove up, the door opened and Henry stepped onto the porch. Next came Lily, her gray bun bobbing in time with her smile. Behind her were Donald and Torger with his wife, Beth. Karl grinned and waved two fingers. Sig held the door for his Olga. Thor, their golden retriever, waved his plume languidly and drew back his lips in a "howdy, pardner" canine grin.

We shook hands with the line of Zillioxes, anchored by Henry. The doorway led directly into the dining room. The table was of a size to accommodate their robust family. Platters and serving dishes covered every part of it: beef, a pork roast, a huge ham, ribs in a sauce still sizzling, fried chicken piled in a golden pyramid. I recognized slabs of pike and steaks from another great fish—sturgeon, as it turned out. There were potatoes boiled, baked, buttered, browned, and mashed. Carrots and string beans, Swiss chard, peas, corn, and a bowl of wild rice. Sweet, dill, and bread-and-butter pickles and pickled beets—all homemade. Another area held desserts: three kinds of pie, puddings, cakes.

There were two place settings on one corner of the table and eight chairs lined up along the walls. Lily waved us to the table.

I had loaded my plate before I made it past the baked beans. Barbara and I sat and waited expectantly for the others to serve themselves, but like the congregation in church when the pastor spreads his hands, the Zillioxes sat in the chairs along the wall. I looked at Henry. He smiled gently and nodded. Donald returned my gaze gravely. Lily mopped her forehead with a hankie. I ate a bite of ham. Torger crossed his legs and stared out the window. Beth sliced off two more slabs of bread and held them out to us. A space opened up on my plate and Lily appeared at my elbow. "You haven't tried the meatloaf, Doctor. It has venison in it."

In all my life I have not eaten such a meal. The food was magnificent, farm-style gourmet. Under the benign surveillance of our hosts, we ate until our stomachs pleaded for mercy. We filled our plates again. Lily flushed with pride.

When at length we departed, an hour late for afternoon office hours, we shook hands in reverse. Thor allowed us to lean on his broad canine shoulders while we waddled to the car. I pushed back the seat a notch and loosened my belt. Barbara opened two buttons on her uniform. She groaned.

"Me, too," I said. "Such grand people, but I don't want to eat again for a week."

Barbara said, "Have you forgotten? Doreen and your fishing buddy, Neil, invited us to supper tonight, that twenty-pound northern pike he caught."

Grace, sincerity, payment in a currency of respect and affection: these were values of the times.

The T. Rex of Throat Infections

BLAINE, the doctor who moved to Trillium during the fourth year of my practice, became my best friend. Two isolated solo practitioners had much to share, and we helped each other when we could, from fifty-five miles apart.

There was no hospital in Trillium. One evening Blaine called to ask if he could bring twelve-year-old Susan to Northpine Hospital. I agreed and, when he arrived, went to see Susan with him. The girl's throat was ghastly, with dirty-white exudates covering her tonsils and soft palate. Neither of us had ever seen anything quite like it. I was dubious about our staffing ability to cope with something that looked so ominous, so we rode together to the newly finished hospital in nearby Koochiching.

Smears taken from the girl's throat showed bacteria that resembled diphtheria. The hospital had no antitoxin on hand; no one had seen diphtheria in decades. We contacted the state health department and they, too, had none in stock. ("Diphtheria? Are you sure?" was the skeptical response we got.) The state people located antitoxin in Chicago, and we were told we could expect to receive it within twenty-four hours.

Susan died twelve hours before it arrived.

Blaine and I were faced with our own private epidemic. We rounded up anyone who would sit still and did throat cultures to send off to the state department of health. The focal point was clearly around Trillium; Blaine had forty-three positive cultures, while I had less than a dozen.

Word got around quickly, as it does in a small community. A couple of evenings into the epidemic, the county nurse and I held a clinic in the high school gymnasium. I gave more than a thousand shots of diphtheria toxoid in a frantic attempt to catch up.

Why Susan? She had had one or two DPT shots as an infant, then had received no others. Where did it come from? Seldom do we learn answers to such questions. No one else died. That was little consolation to Susan's parents.

They Don't Grow 'Em Like They Used To

D URING MY YEARS in practice along Minnesota's northern border, many of my patients were woods workers or commercial fishermen. In my mind, it is a toss-up as to which breed of men was the sturdier. Wresting a living from forest or stormy lake during mosquito-plagued summers or near-arctic winters requires rugged individuals to start with, then hones them to a self-reliant edge.

Take Hjalmer Swanson. It was a busy morning, the waiting room full. Hjalmer sat quietly until his name was called. He hobbled to the exam table and inched up onto it.

"Hurt my ankle, Doc," he said.

I eased off a Sorel winter boot and exclaimed over the puffy soft-tissue swelling it hid. An x-ray showed what we call a trimalleolar fracture: both side tabs of bone stabilizing the joint broken and a chip off the back of the tibia. The man had walked in on it! My previous experience with injuries so severe was of a person stretched supine, justifiably howling in distress.

I apologized for our having made him sit and wait.

"Heck [actually, he used a robust woods-worker word], Doc, felt good to sit down. Hard part was gettin' out of the [strong descriptive word] woods, 'cause the snow's three, four feet deep."

Big Ole was one of those sturdy individuals. He worked for Tom Grotski out west of Sarah Lake, the next village south of Northpine. The train provided transportation for men from the woods. It arrived in Northpine at about 7:00 A.M. on Saturdays to disgorge a gaggle of thirsty jacks. Headed south again on Sunday at about 7:30 P.M., it collected the same fellows, slaked, broke, and subdued. I said "about" for the times because our beloved Northern Pacific Railroad Company did not worry itself excessively about punctuality.

Big Ole was, well, *big*. He could hoist a log on each shoulder and wade to the pulpwood landing through snow that reached his hips. In camp and sober, he had no peer. In town, at the Power House, Northpine's municipal bar, Ole became a lawman's nightmare. (The local police had what they called a "Big Ole Alert," which involved deputizing a couple of strong bodies for back-up.) Ole's usual Saturday-night accommodations were the local lockup cell. It reminded us Northpiners of that chap on the *Andy Griffith Show,* Otis something. The police always released Big Ole on Sunday afternoon, in time to catch the southbound evening train.

The depot was a quarter of a mile west of town. To reach it on foot, one had to walk along a winter-dark road that was one stretched-out S-curve. Ole would lumber along it, arriving just in time to catch his ride back to camp.

One Sunday evening, I received a call from the hospital. "Big Ole," nurse Edna Freeman said.

The man was stretched out on the emergency room table, his feet jutting well past its end.

I asked, "What happened?"

"Hit by a car," Edna said. "He was running down the middle of the road toward the depot, trying to catch the train. With his dark clothes and no street lights, Bob Thompson hit him right between the headlights of his pickup."

I examined Big Ole. Alert, if restive.

"Gotta catch the [strong, descriptive adjective] train, Doc. Lemme outta here."

Scuffs and abrasions. A couple of cuts that would require stitches. A clear liquid seeping from his ears. Cerebral-spinal fluid! X-rays confirmed the presence of a basal skull fracture.

Big Ole was our guest for ten days. We monitored him, shot him full of antibiotics, and did our best to make him stay put. When he left, he conceded that "da foot vas pritty goot, Doc, an' all dem beaut-ful gals what served it, too, by gar!" He of course ignored his appointment for follow-up.

About a year later, I was called to the hospital one Sunday evening. Big Ole. Bruised and battered. Dead.

"What happened?" I asked.

Jonas, the driver of our spanking-new ambulance, said, "Hit by a car, Doc."

I said, "Running down the middle of the road in the dark, toward the depot."

"Yeah. How'd you know?"

"Call it a hunch."

Debbie

I RECEIVED THE CALL one night at 10:30. I kicked aside the covers and lay quietly, caught in the precious sliver of time that hangs suspended between the shattering of peace and the moment when I must respond.

Through a window opening onto spring came a breeze hesitant as a lad's first kiss, air turgid with the perfume of pin cherry blossoms. Frogs in some nearby puddle peeped frantically.

I sighed and dropped one foot to the floor. It found a slipper. The other followed and I was nearly sitting. I shuffled toward the window and pulled aside the shade. A bright splash of stars gleamed from the northland's virgin skies.

The bedside phone jangled again and I heard apology in its ring. Nurse Kathy Parkinson sounded anxious. "Are you coming, Doctor? You need to."

We lived at that time in an apartment in the hospital. Handy. I slogged into the hospital proper, my slippers flapping an instant behind each stride, like an echo. Kathy stood in the emergency room entrance. She beckoned urgently. A teenage girl lay on the gurney. When I saw her face, wistful dreams of sleep fled.

Debbie Klein was sixteen that May evening she decided that she needed to talk. Homer Stevens was her boyfriend, a decent guy, willing to listen. He told me about it while we waited for my surgical nurse, Elaine Andresen, rousted to help in the operating room. Words bubbled out of Homer like water from a hillside spring. Shock.

He said, "We drove around in my old junker Ford. She said she couldn't stand her parents any longer, that they didn't understand her. We ended up out at the old Horekoski place. That's where the county straightened the section-line jog in the road. Me and her, we sometimes park on the abandoned part, talking and . . . stuff. We was smoking . . . now, Doc, don't you tell her folks about that.

"About a quarter mile down, this other guy turned off the new road onto this same stretch we were parked on. He came at us like a bull moose, bouncing over all those chuck holes. Debbie was nestled down against my side. I was beginning to get nervous and sat up straighter, thought for sure he would rip the bottom outta his car. When I realized he wasn't gonna stop, I hollered, 'Duck!' but Deb, she popped up instead, just as that yahoo slammed into us."

Debbie Klein had crashed into and through the windshield of Homer's car. Face first.

Safety glass shatters in a spider-web pattern. Each fragment became a four-sided lancet, and the spider web inscribed itself on her face, a mosaic of skin islands faithful to the bits of glass that had cut them. Like the rings of a grotesque target, they circled and spiraled about her nose and her cheeks, to the line of her chin and into her hair. No single flap of skin was longer than an inch or wider than three-eighths of an inch. Shielded by the buttress of her forehead, her eyes and their lids were spared.

We prepared to operate. I used the finest suture material we had. A routine evolved: morphine, to keep her comfortable; cleanse and drape with sterile towels; inject anesthetic into an area small enough that I could repair it before sensation returned; move to another spot.

That night stays with me: the smell of fresh blood and our own sweat; cramped muscles in my back and shoulders, ignored until, when finally acknowledged, I could scarcely move; the monotony of suturing and tying over and over, with thread so fine my tired eyes could not always find it or my fingers avoid breaking it. Once Elaine nearly fainted and we had to rest for a while.

We worked from 11:00 P.M. until 6:00 in the morning. Debbie looked like the Patchwork Girl from Oz, but her face was again a face, not some horror from a grade-C movie.

Nature has her rules and scar is rarely invisible. Still, I was proud of the results. The lines crisscrossing Debbie's face were like delicate, if premature, wrinkles. Her philosophy was uncomplicated: "I can live with it. Thanks, Doc."

Cora Benson

MISS CORA BENSON stood straight as a tall pine. She marched briskly to the client's chair in my office. Her chart consisted of new, blank pages.

I said, "Tell me a little about yourself."

Her diction was precise, that of someone for whom verbal communication was a lifelong tool. "You have my name. I am seventy-one years old. I retired from my profession of teaching six years ago. I am originally from Minneapolis. I graduated from St. Cloud Teacher's College with a two-year certificate, later earned my degree during summer sessions. I came north decades ago, fell in love with the country and its people. I bore no offspring and have had hundreds of children, all third-graders."

I said, "I see that you live over in Koochiching. What brings you here today?"

"Two things. My symptoms and dissatisfaction with my previous physician."

"Tell me."

"I've been tired for nearly a year. About four months ago, I began to have chest pains. They were vague and ill defined. It took me one month to decide the discomfort was real, a second to work through both my own inertia and Doctor—my previous physician's waiting list, then a third to navigate the maze of medical care."

She straightened and winced, seeming not to notice her response. "My doctor did a physical examination," she said, "then referred me to Dr. Mork in Duluth."

"The psychiatrist?"

"I saw him three times, a week apart. As my pains became sharper, so did he. I believe he considered me insubordinate when his advice produced no results. This past month, at home, I've applied large doses of positive thinking: 'The pain is not there.' The trouble is—"

"It still hurts. Does the pain increase when you breathe?"

"No, it's just there."

"Do you cough?"

"No."

"Do you . . ." I asked my battery of questions.

Barbara was working in the office the day that Cora Benson returned to hear results of her various tests. She laid the chart before me. Clipped to its jacket was the pathology report on the bone marrow sample I had sent to Duluth.

"Oh, no," I said.

Barbara patted my shoulder.

I met Cora Benson at the door. I felt the trembling of her arm as I guided her to the client's chair. I made a show of seating myself, dragging out the seconds. I raised my eyes and met the full impact of her gaze. I tasted familiar dread, gummy on my lips, wishing there was a way to make the task easier, the message more pleasant. I fingered the report.

"Miss Benson, I have here—"

"It shows cancer."

"I'm very sorry. You have a form that originates in the bone marrow. We call it multiple myeloma."

"Thank God."

My face must have registered surprise.

"Not 'thank God it's cancer'; I haven't lost my zest for life. Do you have any idea how frustrating it is to consult a physician, only to realize he has not been listening to half of what you have said and that he disbelieves the rest?"

I pushed her chart aside. "How does that make you feel?"

A tear crept down Cora Benson's cheek. I handed her a box of Kleenex and she dabbed at the salty streak.

"All my life I've tried to be strong. I cherish independence. What will happen if—or is it when—I become disabled? I have long believed that death itself holds no terror, for is it not as much a part of life as birth? Yet, now I find that ... I am afraid."

We talked long past Cora Benson's appointment time. When we emerged from the office, Barbara MacDonald and nurse Elaine Andresen gave me *looks*. Diffidence before the doctor stilled Elaine's tongue, but wives are not so burdened. Barbara followed me back into my now-empty office.

Her eyes had that look about them. "Your patients are in open mutiny out there in the waiting room."

"I was *with* a patient."

"The ones with appointments fifteen, thirty, and forty-five minutes overdue."

"Things come up, Barbara!"

"You made the rule yourself, RAM: 'keep me on schedule.' How can we poor nurses—"

"Can the 'poor nurse' bit. I'm sorry. No, dang it, I'm not. This was an emergency."

"Ardith Moog is out there, and she's waiting to die, too! And Joannie's here with that young hooligan of hers; he fed the fish in your aquarium a bag of potato chips. We nurses have to keep *everyone* happy. Now my eyes are all red. I hope people will think you've been beating me." She giggled, a sob in transition. I drew her into my arms.

"Don't kiss the help!" she said.

I paid her no heed.

"Oh, RAM, there's never enough time! I thought I would get used to people having to die, but—"

"Maybe we don't."

"Maybe we shouldn't," she whispered.

Home Is Home Is Home

HEALTH PROFESSIONALS regard a nursing home as a good idea. Odd that so many *patients* resist entering one. I tried viewing things by shifting my focus 180 degrees: Given a roommate not of your choice, gender the only thing in common. Made to report to a young woman every time you pee or poop. Put to bed and gotten up at the convenience of the staff. Who guarantees those inalienable rights we bring with us to the front door of the place? Which rights *remain* inalienable? I had cause to consider these very issues during my tenure in Northpine.

I had been up the night before: the Bartlett baby, then a heart attack patient. I stepped into the nurses' station of the long-term-care section of the Northpine hospital complex. R.N. Nora Conner was in charge of the unit. She had summoned me for a conference.

She impaled me with a glare that stung. "We have had another 'incident,'" she said.

"I'm tired, my brain slipped out of gear. Was there a previous one?"

"Fosdick Tyrone."

Fosdick. Chronic congestive heart failure. A woodsman's vocabulary. Pleasant old guy, to my observation. I realized Ms. Conner had not ratcheted down her glare.

"I'm sorry to hear—What again was the incident in regards to Mr. Tyrone?"

"My girls caught him doing . . . that thing."

"Ah, yes. Masturbating. As I recall, it was at night, in his own bed, in his own room. He had no intention of involving anyone else."

"It is hardly the kind of thing—"

"Back up. I assume we have another example of the natural activity Mr. Tyrone engaged in that—"

"Doctor! This is not a matter to be brushed aside. You are responsible for seeing that your patients observe the rules of our establishment."

"Ms. Conner, I'm too tired to argue. Who is the latest culprit?"

"Well, it involves—Please speak softly. One of my girls found the door to Gwen Springstone's door closed and when she entered she discovered Amos Friar, from Room 117, in bed with Gwen."

"By mistake?"

"Heavens no. They were—This is difficult. Undressed."

"Ah. I assume your girl knocked before she, uh, barged in."

"They were making love!"

"Really. Not such a bad thing to make. Encouraging to a doctor noticing more gray hairs each day."

"What do you expect us to do in the face of such behavior?"

"I'd suggest that your girl back out and close the door quietly. I hope she did that."

"I was certain that you would fail to back me up. Why, they aren't even married."

"There is that. Look, Gwen's husband died twenty years ago. And I had to comfort Bernice Friar through the last hideous days of her life. Remembering the kind of person she was, I could see her poking Amos on the shoulder and saying, 'Good for you, you old fart.' Have we disposed of this latest incident?"

"Doctor, I find your attitude abominable."

"Well, you're not the first to tell me that. Shall I make it an order? Get you and your girls off the hook? If the door to Gwen Springstone's room is closed, find a 'Do Not Disturb' sign—"

"Doctor!"

"Ms. Conner, I regard you as one of the most talented nurses in our institution. When the day comes that I too must call this place 'home,' I devoutly hope that you will be around to supervise my care. Only, if Barbara and I close the door to our room some afternoon, let us decide how we want to spend our time."

God's Will

I N CASE NO ONE HAS NOTICED, let me point out the following: we physicians are renowned for having opinions. Confining dogmatism to the practice of medicine is challenging for some of my colleagues. All right, for me, too. We expect no back talk when we diagnose and prescribe, and we have been known to turn a tad belligerent when someone questions us.

There is a dilemma here. A doctor unsure of himself quickly forfeits the patient's confidence, yet absolute certainty in medicine is as elusive as in any other human pursuit. I tried to form a partnership with my patient, always remembering that I sometimes had knowledge she didn't. What happens when push comes to shove?

I think of Hal Smith. The year was 1952 and I was in my Northpine office. I entered Room Two. "What can I do for you?" I chirped. Then my sixty-three-year-old patient's appearance registered on me. "Hal, you're so pale. Have you been bleeding?"

The man shook his head dispiritedly. He acknowledged having had black, tarry stools and a history of ulcers and that he had been experiencing pain typical of an ulcer.

After a few revealing lab tests, I returned to Mr. Smith. "You're bleeding from someplace in your intestines, Hal, heavily, and probably from an ulcer. Your hemoglobin is only five grams, a third of what it should be. I'm putting you in the hospital, and I have several donors coming in. We'll replace—"

The man roused from his lethargy, concern on his face. "What are donors?"

"Blood donors. We need to transfuse you."

"No!" Hal was now fully attentive. "No blood."

"Why not, for God's sake?"

Hal smiled his pale, sad smile. "You said it, Doctor."

The day crept along in concert with the steady, silent, unseen drip of Hal's vital fluid. Four and a half grams. Three grams. Two-point-seven. Pallor so extreme it rendered Hal's flesh white marble. Steadily, dreadfully, a man's life seeping away.

I called a surgeon in Duluth. "He won't allow blood?" my friend asked. "Boy. He might not even make it down here. How could I operate without transfusing him?"

Hal solved that dilemma by refusing to go to Duluth. His son explained, "Down there they'd put him under, then shoot him full of blood, either that or one of those things they make out of blood. He isn't going."

When I sputtered, Hal's son smiled, a reflection of his father.

I became a madman. Vitamin K. Fluids containing salt and sugar. Even, in desperation, a heavy dose of estrogen (what had that salesman said about its ability to slow bleeding?). Antacids and milk by mouth. When summoned, the man's religious counselor provided me with another target for frustration, but nothing more therapeutic from my point of view. His family divided sharply and loudly, but Hal prevailed.

Throughout all that endless day and into early evening the somber drama swirled around Hal Smith.

8:00 P.M.: Hemoglobin two-point-four grams. Impossible.

8:10 P.M.: Hal smiled at me, and died.

I retreated to the refuge of the nursing desk, stared at charts verifying what I had just seen, signed papers making those events official.

I threw the pen across the hallway.

Rena McDoud

I RECALL ASSIGNING the word "contained" to her aspect: the set of her shoulders, her hands clinging to each other, her guarded look. Feature by feature she could hardly have been called beautiful, yet I also remember thinking that my opinion might change if she would only smile. She was thirty-seven years old and looked, well, thirty-seven. Unremarkable.

I had first seen her in the emergency room for vague abdominal pains. I worked her up in the usual fashion but found no lurking disasters. I recorded her affect as "subdued." After the exhaustive studies the symptom of abdominal pain requires so that a physician can be sure he is not overlooking something serious, I sent her on her way with a verbal pat on the head.

She returned to the office two months later. Her symptoms: intractable pain in the abdomen. I could palpate spasms in her colon—so-called spastic bowel—a virtual hallmark of stress. I realized that I had shortchanged a detailed history, indeed, had failed in a doctor's duty to *listen*.

I said, "Tell me about yourself, Mrs. McDoud."

A quick glance, assessing. "That's hard to answer," she said. I sat quietly. "I'm not that special." I said nothing. "I . . . am a widow."

"Tell me about that."

"Hiram died four years ago."

"Hmm."

"He was a wonderful man." Another quick peek at me. "I

miss him. A great deal. I know you said my symptoms are due to stress, but that was four years ago and I've only been sick, the pains, for six months."

"Did anything change six months ago?"

"No." She bent her head and peered at her hands. "Not unless . . . Albert is two years younger than I."

I nodded.

"I see his eyes all the time."

I perked up. "Albert's?"

"Hiram's. He didn't always have to say anything."

"You see Hiram's eyes?"

"That sounds crazy. But then, I'm crazy. After what I did, he had the right to look at me that way."

I squinted at her.

"I don't actually *see* his eyes," she said, "just know they are watching me."

Uh-oh. "Tell me."

"He always said, 'Once a harlot, always a harlot.' He forgave me, but afterward, all he had to do was look at me."

"Yes?"

"I put his picture away, in the drawer. Sometimes I can't remember exactly what he looks like anymore, then I have to— The picture—"

"Let me see if I understand. While Hiram was alive, did you become involved with another man?"

"Hiram had high ideals. Very good ones, I'm sure, but it was hard for anyone else. He would be so angry. After what I did with John, it's understandable. I can hear his voice sometimes."

"Uh—"

"Oh, not really. Just the way it sounded when he was disciplining me."

"Tell me about Albert."

"He is so . . . I like the word 'serene.' Kind. Never carps. He wants to marry me, but . . ."

"But what?"

"Well, I'm still a harlot."

"Whoa. Have I got this straight? Hiram was strict?" She nodded. "And you found solace in a relationship?"

"But I was married."

"And he started calling you that old-fashioned name for slut? How did that make you feel?"

For a moment a spark glinted in her eyes, but she said, "I deserved—"

"Now you have found a gentle man who must care for you as you are."

"Yes, but he doesn't deserve someone like—"

I slapped the desk. "I regard lifelong guilt to be bull crap. You have my permission to borrow that idea."

There was no question about the gleam in her eye now. It stayed.

"Where is your Hiram buried?" I asked.

The gleam disappeared behind lowered lids.

"He isn't exactly buried."

"Pardon?"

"He wanted to be cremated, have me scatter his ashes out along the river."

"And when did you do that?"

"I haven't, actually. They're in an urn on my mantle."

"Hiram's ashes are in your living room?"

"I meant to take them out there, but something held me back."

"What?"

"Well, that harlot—"

"Bull."

"What do you know? I was guilty—"

"Bull."

"You insufferable egotist!"

"Good for you. You're mad and you expressed it. How do you feel toward Hiram?"

"Well, he was always right, so—"

"Bull."

"So—damn you—if he was always right—"

"Bull."

"But if he wasn't *always* right—"

"Now you've got it."

"Then maybe I'm not—"

"You're on track."

"Maybe I should take his ashes out to the river."

I was right: she *was* beautiful when she smiled. She bounded up and squeezed my hand. Feeling returned to my fingers later that afternoon.

She sent me a card a month or so later: an announcement of her engagement to be married.

So, What Is Mental Illness?

CLARA WAS A RELATIVE of a Northpine couple. She lived in a state further south. Diagnosed as having schizophrenia, she had spent a couple of years in a mental institution. One day, the woman's sister asked me if I would consent to having her moved to Northpine, to the long-term-care wing of our hospital. I was dubious, but the woman was convincing, so I agreed to try it out.

Clara was middle-aged, nondescript in appearance, and docile. She turned out to be no problem for our nursing staff. She was receiving no medications, which was unusual in the nightmare world of schizophrenia.

It happened that David, a medical student from the University of Minnesota, had been assigned to my solo-practice office for a year's exposure to rural medicine. He was bright, and I wanted to give him as broad an experience as possible. One day, while making rounds in the long-term-care unit, we interviewed Clara. David was intrigued, so we set up weekly visits, each lasting one-half to three-quarters of an hour. She was pleasant, would periodically pick imaginary objects out of the air, sometimes answered questions with vague, listless responses. We became comfortable with each other.

One day I realized that she would occasionally look directly at me, what I used to call "connecting." On an impulse I cannot explain to this day, I blurted out, "Clara, why do you act crazy when you're not?"

She stopped picking her invisible flowers and gave me a stare as direct as a beam of light.

The upshot? She never again picked air flowers, she began responding to questions rationally, she resumed caring for her appearance, and after a month of what I had to call normality, she went home.

Was she ever schizophrenic? If so, where did it go, and how? Was her label enough to keep her in the hospital?

I wish I knew.

Helen

I STOOD BY A WINDOW IN MY OFFICE, staring out into the gloom of a Northpine April day. Rain fell with dreary persistence to run down window glass in a shimmering shield. It bounced off sodden earth and turned the surface of every puddle into a hedgehog of brief watery spikes. I said to my office nurse, Elaine Andresen, "This is the first time in weeks the waiting room has been empty."

She shrugged. "You'd better get used to it, RAM. This country is a swamp. Okefenokee of the north."

Northpine was in the throes of "mud vacation," that unscheduled disruption of commerce, travel, and school brought on by a combination of rain and the final thawing of pervasive muck. School closed when the first bus mired to the bottom of its frame on some county road; it resumed when the bus could be retrieved.

The telephone rang and Elaine reported on the call. "Helen Haseltine is on the line. She's eight weeks pregnant, having cramps and bleeding. She says she can't get here on her own and thinks she needs help. Will you come?"

Miscarriage—spontaneous abortion, an "ab" in medical jargon—is the fate of up to twenty percent of pregnancies, nature's way of reducing the number of ill-starred babies.

I alerted Barbara to join me and gathered an assortment of sterile supplies. There is always a tinge of excitement when leaving on a country call: the uncertainty, the sometimes primitive environs, medically speaking. I planned contingencies until Barbara said, "Why don't you just wait until we see what's happening?" Practical Barbara.

Fred and Helen Haseltine lived twelve miles west of Northpine on the banks of murky little Muskrat River. Fred was a logger, a hard-working man whom misfortune regarded as a favorite son: his truck threw a piston rod or spilled its load of logs, or prices fell the year he borrowed to buy an extra forty of stumpage. This rainy day, his car was non compos.

Muskrat River Road pointed straight as a surveyor wearing hip boots could mark it. The road was dirt, of course, a modest manmade dike rising above the surrounding muck. Rain and thawing had transformed it into goo that brought to mind primordial ooze. We dropped into ruts that ran like indented railroad tracks down the center of the road. One pair. Muskrat River Road was intended for two-way traffic. If we were to meet another car, we'd be stuck. I stopped a few hundred yards beyond the end of the pavement. When I tried to open my door for a closer inspection, I could not swing it past ridges of mud.

Barbara had that look on her face. "We'd better go back."

Pioneer ancestors and Hippocrates peered over my shoulder. "We'll go on," I said firmly.

I had never heard Barbara use the expression she did then, just before she clamped her lips tight.

We drove the twelve miles in low gear, lurching through mud, plowing through small lakes that hid their depth. At times ruts jerked the steering wheel from my grasp; once it whacked my finger so hard it went numb.

I stopped opposite Fred Haseltine's house and looked at Barbara. "We'll have to leave the car here."

She squinted through sheets of rain at the house, fifty yards away. There was an icy calm to her voice when she said, "You obviously intend to buy me another uniform."

My voice resonated with soothing reasonableness. "Why don't you stay here until I find out what's going on?" She crossed her arms silently.

I plodded through the mud of Fred Haseltine's driveway. It contained a greater proportion of slippery, black, loon-shit muck than the road. Fortunately, I fell only once. I observed protocol and went to the back door. (North woods front doors are always sealed against the cold.) Fred opened it immediately, his gnarled features anxious and tight. Thawed mustiness and decades of wood smoke permeated the place. I crossed the worn kitchen linoleum, sidled past a massive oak dining set—heritage from first-settler parents—and came into a living room darkened by time and squinting windows that rationed light.

Helen Haseltine hunched over in an old wooden rocking chair. "Hi, Doc." Her lips thinned and she froze into disciplined stoicism. Sweat appeared on her forehead. She relaxed and tried to smile. "Hurts; comes and goes."

I asked, "When was your last period?"

"February. Been meaning to come in." She bent over her fists again.

When the pang had passed, I asked, "Is there someplace where I could do a pelvic exam?"

Helen Haseltine rocked her chair and propelled herself to her feet. "The couch."

A piece of biological tissue was trapped in the opening to her womb. The pregnancy was doomed and the uterus needed to be cleaned out. "I'll take you to town," I said. I glanced at Fred. "I can't turn into your driveway."

He said, "I could pull you out of those ruts, get you headed back. Only thing, my truck's down and my tractor bust an axle."

"How am I going to get turned around?"

Fred helped Helen pull a poncho over her head. "Maybe you ain't going to, Doc."

"What if I meet another car? I sweated that all the way out here."

Fred opened the door onto the sodden world outside. "I don't know how to say this, Doc, but, uh, well, no one else would be fool enough to try. No hard feelings."

We backed the twelve miles into Northpine. I mired down once, squeezed through the narrow crack my door allowed, hung up on mud as it was, and shoveled enough sand into the rut to get traction. We encountered no cars. My neck was sore for a week from craning over my shoulder to drive, a position that at least spared me the sight of steam boiling off the overheated radiator.

At the hospital I removed the dead products of conception from Helen's uterus. "I'm sorry," I said.

She dried her cheek with her palm. "You wonder, would the kids have had a sister or a brother."

I patted her on the shoulder. "I could let you go back home."

She chuckled, a sound watery as the weather outside. "Are you going to take me?"

I admitted her to the hospital for the night, but not without a pang of guilt. Like most of her neighbors, could she afford the $7.50-a-day expense?

Pudge Dalafus

IN RETROSPECT, it was oddly like an omen, our game that evening. I inspected daughter Jane gravely: cowgirl hat, skirt adorned with spangles and leather tassels, a velveteen vest. I wondered if my love shone as brightly as I felt it. Seven is so special.

Jane asked, "Do you like my Dale Evans costume?"

"Who is he?" I asked.

She rolled her eyes. My word, her mother in diminutive form. "Daddy, Dale isn't a he, he's a she. She's in movies and married to Roy Rogers and Trigger."

"Two at once? That's called bigamy."

"No! He's a horse."

"Dale's a horse?"

"No—Mom, make Daddy don't do that."

My wife looked up from a book and did an excellent imitation of a daughter imitating a mother rolling her eyes.

I said, "Do you want me to be Trigger for a while?"

Son Allan ran at me from his height of two years. "Ride?"

Jane said, "I'm Dale and I get to and you're too small."

Trigger said, "You first Dale Evans, then Allan."

I dropped to hands and knees and Jane landed astride my back. Allan bellowed, his eyes screwed shut in his Campbell's Soup pixie face.

I said, "Miss Evans, I hear a dogie, lost and lonesome. Hang on while we investigate." I rolled him around with one hand—

front hoof—and picked him up about the middle.

"Giddy up." She dug in her heels and I was glad her costume did not include spurs. "Faster."

"You have top speed, Miss Evans."

Allan screamed, "Ride!"

"Hold him in front of you, Jane," I said.

"Oh, okay."

"Ride." Allan was all damp smiles.

Trigger said, "Groan."

The telephone rang.

"Don't go," Jane whispered.

"Not unless I have to."

My wife held out the receiver, her somber eyes challenging. I rolled onto my side to cradle the receiver against my ear, sending my riders into a giggling heap.

Nurse Edna Freeman said, "We need you in the emergency room."

"Can it wait?"

"I think you should come, Doctor."

Barbara banged the receiver in place and scowled into her book.

Allan said, "Ride?"

Dale Evans tossed her hat onto a chair and went to Jane's room.

I trudged toward the hospital.

Pudge Dalafus lay supine on the emergency room table. He sparkled. Flecks of brilliance, reflections from the overhead spotlight, gleamed in his hair and his clothing, from his face, eyelids, and ears. I bent over the man. His sequins were specks of pulverized glass.

"Pudge, what happened?"

"That you, Doc? Can't open my eyes. Don't know. Driving home to my place out in New Bavaria Township. Dark night, but nothing wrong with my eyesight. A car was coming toward me, swinging a little from side to side. Still rods away, though. Those county roads are dirt and narrow, so I was over to my side, careful-like.

"All the sudden, there's this explosion in my face and my windshield is ground glass. I ended up in the ditch, all this stuff in my eyes."

Edna Freeman peered over my shoulder while I tried to sponge up glass sand. She said, "We need a vacuum cleaner."

"Good idea. Run next door and ask Barbara for her Electrolux."

It worked like a salesman's promise in those places accessible. I syringed grit from his eyes and he blew glass dust from his nose.

"Still can't figure what happened," he muttered.

Memory poked me in the ribs: the time Sig Worth had hit a deer that came through the windshield at him. "Any deer, Pudge?"

"No deer. I know deer."

I grinned. Northpiners considered Pudge the third best poacher in the county, a significant honor in a land of individualists like ours. We rated Abe Quick as having a slight edge on Pudge. Of course, no one contended with Father Julian for the number one spot. I hesitate to reveal this, but the truth must be told. Thing is, he was so blatant about it.

The exploded windshield loomed as a mystery.

When I had finished with Pudge, I found Petr Brueger sitting in the waiting room, hunched over with his usual somber scowl.

Pudge and Petr were best friends. They lived on adjoining farms and had arrived in our area within six months of each other, Petr from "da alt con-try," Pudge from West Palm Beach, Florida. Pudge and Petr, an improbable pair.

I detoured and went to sit beside him. "Pudge will be out soon," I said. "Can you give him a ride home? I suppose his car is undrivable." I massaged Petr's shoulder. "He's fine."

Petr shook his head. "*Nicht* fine."

"A little scratched up but nothing serious."

"*Er ist toten.*"

"Killed? No, Petr, he's alive and kicking."

"Doc, why you make kidding with me? This *gibt mir* very sad."

I squinted at the gnarled little man. "I swear to you that he is okay, won't even need to stay in the hospital."

Petr had one eye that tracked to the side, white and useless. He turned it on me.

"No good, Doc, dead *toten*. He let me ride him."

"Uh, pardon?"

"Bareback *und mit* no reins."

I think my voice squeaked a little. "Pudge?"

"*Ja, auch Pudge toten.*"

I rubbed my temples. "What are you talking about? Pudge is in one piece."

"I hope so, Doc, so I can sue that *Schweinhund* broke."

"Sue Pudge? I thought he was your friend."

"*Ja, das ist richtig*, WAS. I sue him for tousand dollar. Five tousand. No mercy for what he done."

"What *did* he do?"

"He killed Fritz."

"Who the blazes is Fritz?"

"*Mein Pferd.*"

"Your *horse?* How? When?"

"Tonight, he ran him into. *Tot*, dead in the ditch he left him."

Deputy sheriff Roger Edwards later put the pieces together for me. Petr Brueger had set out that dark evening in his old, pedigreed International Harvester pickup truck, herding Fritz ahead of him along County Road 9. Fritz was a large chestnut draft horse, broad and sturdy. The color of his coat rendered him virtually invisible, even in the lights of an oncoming car. If a driver did not know that he should be on a Fritz alert, he wouldn't see him coming.

Fritz trotted ahead of the truck, meandering from shoulder to shoulder, contained by water-filled ditches on either side. The animal was one hundred yards ahead of Petr when Pudge happened along. A half- to three-quarters ton of rearing horse makes short work of both windshield and animal.

The lawsuit? Perhaps Pudge's counter suit for damage to his car cancelled Petr's. At least, Northpine heard no more about it.

When I returned home that evening, Jane and Allan were in bed. I thought that Dale Evans was still awake, but when Trigger whispered his regrets, she turned over and faced the wall.

Have you ever wished life gave second chances?

Office Hours

AT THE END OF ANOTHER DAY of seeing office patients, I picked up that bane of a doctor's existence, a dictation microphone. Time to record observations and opinions.

First case:

I persisted gently. "I'm not doubting your word, Mrs. Prodzig. I'm as puzzled as you are. You've been on a 1200-calorie diet for three months now, and in that time your weight has gone from—let's see—218 pounds to 229. I have no explanation."

Forty-year-old Hortense Prodzig, homemaker and mother of three, stared at me damp-eyed. "I want to be slim, Doctor, but my body just wants to be fat. Why, I can't even eat all you prescribed on that ishy diet. By the time I finish supper, then have to sit there and choke down your horrid 1200 calories . . ."

I reached for another chart.

The young woman sitting in the client's chair was smartly dressed, befitting her profession of legal secretary. "Attractive," "intelligent," and "sensitive" completed my summation of her attributes. She was a diagnostic conundrum, causing referral-time confusion.

I said, "Betty, this is the third time in two months that I've done a pelvic examination and checked for infection, and again

I find nothing wrong. Tell me one more time about this malodorous discharge."

"I have an odor all the time, Doctor, and nothing seems to change it. I cleanse and take precautions." She shook her head helplessly. "I don't know what else to say."

"Forgive me, Betty. Today I paid particular attention and I could smell nothing. Can you describe the odor in words?"

"I don't smell anything, Doctor."

"I don't understand."

"It's my husband. Every time he comes near, he tells me I stink."

Mentally I tore up my referral letter. "Tell me how things are between you and your husband."

I reached for a third chart.

A form clipped to the front gave the patient's name and her age of sixty-nine. I said, "I see you're here for a physical to renew your driver's license."

"Oh no, Doctor, I'm taking driving lessons. I've never had a license."

"Good for you. What led you to decide such a thing at this time of life?"

"My mother—she's eighty-eight—just finished the beginner's course and I'll be darned if I'm going to let her get ahead of me."

Let's see, chart number four.

I finished taking a Pap smear and stood beside the examination table. "Everything is just fine, Mrs. Johnson. A small erosion of the cervix, of no consequence." I retreated to the corner sink behind the curtain shielding Mrs. Johnson and washed my hands.

I heard her say to nurse Elaine Andresen, "I *told* my husband he was going to wear that out."

Chart number five:

Oh, yes, the Kramers. Ivar, the ostensible patient, was back for a recheck. Theirs was one of those tales to warm the cockles of your heart. (Odd: I don't recall from Anatomy 101 a structure named "cockle.") Ivar's stroke had wiped out Broca's speech center and therefore his entire vocabulary. His wife, Addie, taught second grade. She brought home reading primers and Ivar waded through *See Spot Run* for the second time in his life. It worked. I often wondered: did Broca's area recover, or did the right side of his brain learn what the left side had surrendered?

Chart number six:

Two teen-aged youngsters sat side by side in Room Three. I chirped, "Miss Kathy Jones? This record says you are the patient. What seems to be the matter?"

She mumbled, "Tit bit."

"Pardon?"

Kathy's gaze raked the pimply boy beside her. "You tell 'im."

He flushed so red I fancied I felt radiant heat. "Well, like . . . see, we uns was ridin' in the back seat of Wilbur's car, like, an' he went over a bump real hard and . . . that's how Kathy got her tit bit."

Then there was Rita. Her chart, when I removed it from the holder beside the door to Room Two, was filled with the blank pages that meant "new patient." She lived in a neighboring community.

Two women sat in chairs beside my small desk. The older had that worn and resigned look; one of life's foot scrapers, I decided. The young woman, huddled so tightly at her side as to appear an appendage, was a startling echo: a late-teens daughter and her mother.

I sat facing them. "Who's the patient?"

Mother jerked a thumb. "She is."

I looked at the younger woman. "What's your name?"

Mother said, "She's Rita Antonelli."

I spoke to Rita. "What seems to be wrong?"

"She doesn't feel good."

Pointedly, I continued talking to Rita. "Please tell me in your own words what brings you here today."

Mother said, "She's been sick to her stomach and her monthlies is messed up."

I inspected Mother. "I need to get the facts from Rita. How old are you?"

"She's seventeen."

I stood up. "Mrs. Antonelli, I want you to give my receptionist some more information. Come with me. No, Rita, you stay here."

An hour, a few pointed questions, and a physical examination later, I again sat across from Rita and a puzzled Mrs. Antonelli. I said, "Rita asked me to let you know her condition. She's pregnant—three months along—and she's doing well."

"But she isn't married."

Sudden radiance lit Mrs. Antonelli's face. "Holy Mother of God, the second Immaculate Conception!"

. . .

And, finally, Frances Olson. She was plump and comfortable, the archetypal pastor's wife, beloved by family and congregation.

I said, "You are forty-two? And there's something funny about your right breast? Six months?"

Mrs. Olson was endowed with large, pendulous breasts. The right one was half again the size of the left: hard, red with violent, consuming inflammation, an open area of drainage, swollen masses in the right axilla. No microscopic examination was necessary to make a diagnosis of deadly accuracy. Cancer. So-called "inflammatory" in type, indicating a raging course. Virtually untreatable, it was obviously widespread.

My eyes were tortured when I could look at Mrs. Olson.

She sighed. "I thought so. That's why I didn't come sooner." She struggled to a sitting position, wincing when the weight of her traitorous breast tugged at painful nerves.

She said, "My husband is a good man. He has his calling and he'll get by. My children are two wonderful kids. I've had them for seventeen and fifteen years. They'll adjust after I'm gone. There's just one thing, though." She looked at me with haunted eyes. "In our congregation, there's no one else who can play the organ."

Midge

THE PRACTICE OF OBSTETRICS provides a doctor with some of medicine's greatest joys, and with some of its most daunting challenges.

Colleen Kocinski was as Irish as a begorra. She bubbled with joy and innocent zest the way dark ale tickles. I saw her in my office one afternoon, her first visit. "We live over in Koochiching," she said. "Vlad works in the paper mill. We have eleven children. God has been so good to us! I'm here to see about baby."

I glanced around, puzzled. She laughed and patted her generous abdomen. "Number twelve, he's still in. I suppose you'll want my duds off." I handed Colleen Kocinski a gown and went into the hall while she changed.

I said, "Once more, Mrs. Kocinski—"

"Oh, Doctor," she said, "no one calls me that. Just Colleen."

I smiled. "Try again to remember your last period."

She compressed her lips and scanned the ceiling, then shook her head and chuckled. "It's no use. I never keep track of those things. We take whatever God gives us."

I said, "On the basis of size and when you felt life, I vote for five to five-and-a-half months along."

Colleen's labor began without warning or obvious cause at twenty-eight or -nine weeks. Her bag of waters broke and there was no turning back. She lay on our delivery table, her sparkle dimmed. I studied her: gray at forty-three, her round face bearing worry lines that cut across cheer. "Can you stop it, Doctor?" she asked.

"There's no way. Besides, we don't dare now that you have lost fluid."

"Baby's still so small."

I tried to coax concern off my face. "I'd send you to Duluth—"

"I wouldn't make it," she said. "It won't be long."

"I'll do the best I can."

"It's ready, Doctor." I slid into the gown held by nurse Edna Freeman and pulled on gloves. Colleen peered at me between her legs. "Okay?" She pushed.

The baby she expelled was a squirrel-sized little girl, her skin transparent with prematurity, hands no bigger than nickels, spindly arms and legs. In 1953, neonatal intensive care units were not even a gleam in the eye of some far-sighted pediatrician, and babies born at less than thirty weeks did not live.

I held the limp icon of a person in my left hand and wiped her face gently with a gauze 4×4. Her eyelids popped open. I jackknifed her thin legs against her abdomen. Her blue eyes crossed and she coughed, a puff of sound. I squeezed her chest and released it. She raised her arms in an indignant startle position.

"Hey, little lady," I whispered into my mask. Little lady blinked. I used a bulb syringe to suck out her mouth and nose. She pushed back with her tongue and gagged grotesquely. Her hands became fists; she kicked me in the biceps and screwed up her face. Her first cry was a squeak. She bleated twice and began to scream Polish-Irish at me as fast as she could gulp in air.

The effect on Colleen was electric. "It's alive? Let me see. A girl! Thank God . . . but so small. Is she all right? Will she live?

You must do something—Baptize her. Please, now. I don't want her to die before she—We can't take a chance."

"Colleen, I'm not a priest."

"God will understand. Please do it for me." She raised herself up onto her elbows. "I'll tell you what to say—Get some water—"

I carried the squirming infant in my left hand and pushed a wheeled stand with its basin of sterile water toward the head of the delivery table. She dipped her hand. "I baptize you," she said, "in the name of Jesus Christ. Amen."

"Amen," I said softly.

Colleen smiled and relaxed. Two-and-a-half pound Girl Kocinski piddled on my arm.

In the nursery, we placed a gooseneck lamp to shine down on Girl Kocinski. Barbara MacDonald came to see me. "Our smallest rubber nipple is twice too large."

I sighed. "She doesn't need food this first night. Warmth. Oxygen. Monitoring." A miracle, I thought. "Until she, uh—"

Barbara had on her stubborn look. "Until she what?"

"Well, dies."

"She won't."

"Barbara, you know the odds." I dug out my textbooks and showed her the facts. I spent time with Colleen, preparing her. She cried without restraint.

Barbara muttered, "She won't."

Barbara set up a cot in our tiny nursery beside Girl Kocinski's bassinet. She and Edna Freeman worked out alternating shifts. They solved the problem of too-large nipples by sliding a short piece of lab pipette tubing onto the end of a medicine dropper. Sugar water, a drop at a time.

Girl Kocinski was still alive in the morning. She breathed with brief pants that barely stirred her chest.

Barbara said, "She doesn't suck." I shook my head and squeezed her shoulder. She stiffened and pulled away. "She'll learn how, but for now—she doesn't."

"Then we'd better gavage her." I found a small, soft rubber catheter and slid it into Girl Kocinski's stomach. Her protests were subdued, her cry a soft mewing.

"She *won't*," Barbara said. I saw a tear on her cheek. "Her color's good." Pale to my eyes, through that cellophane skin.

For a doctor, life delivers a steady supply of new patients. I moved past the sadness of Girl Kocinski, comforted Colleen as best I could, and sent her home. For hours at a time I forgot our midget baby while I helped those more robust. I missed Barbara, cloistered in our cramped nursery. Each night I slept with the expectation of a call from her: "It's happened, RAM."

Girl Kocinski lost weight: two-and-a-half pounds; two pounds, three ounces; two pounds, one ounce. On the fourth day Barbara said, "I think she can suck again." I pulled out the gavage tube. "I'm mixing Colleen's breast milk more that half and half now."

I hugged Barbara. "When are you coming home?" Giving up, I thought.

"She's going to make it." I left my books on the shelf.

I made rounds on the seventh morning. Barbara waved urgently at me through the nursery window. Head to forehead, she and Colleen Kocinski huddled over the bassinet. Oh God, time? My pulse jumped. I tied on a mask and went to peer over Barbara's shoulder.

Girl Kocinski blinked at me, cross-eyed, and jerked her arms and legs in a dog-paddle pattern. She demonstrated her nuzzling reflex, her mouth gaping like a baby robin's. Barbara said, "Watch." Girl Kocinski attacked the rubber tip of the medicine dropper, sucking with the single-minded intensity of a hungry and experienced baby.

I said, "My God."

Barbara's chortle was triumphant.

"She's really drinking," I said.

"Of course."

"I believe she's going to make it."

"Of *course*."

I pulled Barbara's head against my side for a moment and kissed her hair. Colleen winked at me and said, "You can have her back pretty soon, Doctor."

One month later, Midge went home to the loving bedlam of the Kocinski household.

Curbstone Consultations

THE NORTHPINE POST OFFICE serves two functions: first, that conceived by old Ben Franklin and, second, as a community meeting place. In a village without door-to-door mail delivery, if you hang around the post office for a day you will see the neighbors, town politicians, a distant cousin. Everyone will come by.

One day as I hurried into the small brick building, Olaf Tallifson spied me. "Ho, Doc!" he boomed.

"Olaf," I said as I tossed throw-aways into the wastebasket.

"Got a minute?" he called.

"I'm late at the office."

"Got this here pain, Doc. Starts in the back, spreads into—You wouldn't want me to say, here in the open like this."

"That's true, Olaf. Call the office and make an appointment."

"It's one them private places."

"My receptionist, Elaine Andresen, will be glad to give you a time."

I scooted out the door just as Jeremiah Blizzard swooped around the corner in his functioning Model A Ford. I waited. His driving was erratic and it paid to give him leeway. Olaf caught me by the near arm, I with one foot raised to step off the curb. "What d'you think it is, Doc?"

"Hard to say, Olaf. Make an appointment."

Olaf tightened his grip. "Got this little sore on my lip."

"I need to run."

"It won't take a minute, Doc. I just want to know if it's serious."

"Appointment!"

"When old Doc Hargrave was here he never bothered with appointments."

"I'll see you." I tugged at my arm.

"You ain't said about my pain." He glanced about, pointed discreetly.

I returned my orphan leg to the sidewalk. "That'll be three dollars, Olaf."

"What?"

"Consultation fee."

"Heck, Doc, I just asked, friendly-like."

"Three dollars."

Olaf backed away. "I think I'll run on down to Duluth."

There were churches from four denominations in Northpine. While they had some theological differences, competition only blossomed openly and fiercely when it came to community church suppers. A person could munch his way from payday to payday by keeping track of which church was serving what when.

Barbara and I had just seated ourselves for supper at a table in the basement of the Lutheran church. A feminine voice came from a point above my left ear. The woman behind the voice took the chair beside me and I winced. Margery Atkins was forty-nine years old and gifted with a staggering array of self-diagnosed maladies. Time had proved her to be a talented solicitor of curbstone consultations. She stared determinedly at my left ear.

"I have this fierce pain in my stomach."

"Oh?" I ate one of Fannie Swenson's meatballs. Ambrosia.

"On and off for five years."

"Ah?" The scalloped potatoes were delicious.

"A knife runs across my stomach and into my gizzard."

I said, "Barbara, please pass the chicken."

"Something grinds in there."

"I see." I chewed a piece of ham thoughtfully. "Mrs. Koski, did you prepare this delicious sauce?"

"Doctors never find anything. Chiropractors do."

"Good."

"But they don't help either."

"A pity. Luke, can you reach the coffee?"

"Do you believe in chiropractors?"

"Devoutly." I tried Tina's Jell-O salad.

"What's wrong with my gizzard?"

"I believe you . . . have a pain in it." I reached for a chocolate brownie.

Margery Atkins considered, her eyebrows twisted into a question mark. "I want your professional opinion."

I sipped coffee. "That's something I'd be happy to provide you with. Make an appointment with Elaine Andresen, my receptionist."

"I tried but couldn't get one until the next day."

"I'm sorry. When was that?"

"Two years ago. Couldn't wait for something that important."

I said, "Mrs. Atkins, you have been badly treated." I turned to my fellow diners. "Do you suppose we could clear this end of the table? I hope you won't mind. Mrs. Atkins, if you would slip off your things. Right up here—Mrs. Atkins! Where are you going?"

My wife didn't speak to me for the better part of a week. But then, neither did Mrs. Atkins.

Anne

I N 1950 I WAS still practicing with Sam Hargrave, learning
from his experienced example. Sam had taken a weekend off,
leaving me in charge at Northpine Hospital. His patient, eight-
year-old Anne Ryan, was in Room Two for treatment of an acute
sinus infection. Nurse Edna Freeman called me back to the hospital on that Saturday afternoon after Anne had eaten lunch.
"She's unresponsive. Hurry!"

Anne Ryan had plunged from wakefulness to a deep coma
in the space of ten minutes. Eye signs and neurological find-
ings suggested that the infection in her sinuses had penetrated
the thin layer of bone separating her brain from septic nasal
chambers: a brain abscess. I drew blood for cultures, did a spinal tap, found cells in the spinal fluid, and ordered what was for
the times a massive dose of penicillin. For good measure—out
of desperation—I added Streptomycin.

Anne needed a specialist's care. We had no ambulance in
those days. I recall one seriously injured woodsman who arrived stretched out in the box of a battered pickup truck. Jimmy
Nelson was the mortician, and we sometimes used his hearse
to transport sick or injured patients. There was no ready alternative within 100 miles. I called Jimmy at his home; he was out
of town. Sweat poured down my face. Anne was as sick as ever.
Get her to Duluth.

At that time I owned a 1947 Ford two-door sedan. By the removal of a cotter pin, the right front seat came loose and could be laid back, and the vehicle served as an ambulance of sorts. I had transported patients from all around the county to North-pine using my car in this fashion.

We loaded Anne into the car, her head beside me on the passenger seat, her feet in the back. The shortest way to Duluth was to head east on County Highway 64; it saved twenty miles from a distance that was otherwise 185 miles. The problem: it was mud-vacation time, when any unpaved roads were quagmires that sank a vehicle to its hubcaps. I would have to go the long way, through Koochiching.

I drove at speeds up to one hundred miles an hour, praying for some highway patrolman to spot me and provide an escort. They must have been on coffee break. Beside me, little Anne gurgled and slumbered on, an IV spilling more penicillin into her veins. We reached the hamlet of Orr, and she stopped breathing. I pulled to the side of the road and hung my head in despair. To lose a child—

She gave a tiny gasp. Again. Another, and she had resumed breathing. I threw the Ford into gear and resumed my kamikaze trip. Anne began to mumble just as I topped the hill above Duluth, and at St. Andrews Hospital, as we transferred her onto a gurney, she raised her head and looked around. Thank God for penicillin, and for her tiger will to live.

Anne recovered with only minor residual muscle weakness. She stops to see me once in a while when she returns up north.

Thor

WALT BERGER SAID, "You can't put a minute back on the clock. Some things when they happen . . ." He clenched his jaw until the muscles bunched like oysters. I left Thor Voldheim's bedside to put a hand on Walt's shoulder. "We have to wait. Why don't you tell exactly what occurred."

"Gray," Walt said, "his face is so gray."

Gray, like the November sky I could see through the window, the hurrying clouds with their huddled shoulders, the very air scrabbling at trees and slamming against the hospital in gusts to rattle window glass. Like gray-looking sheets on a gray metal bed with gray-handled windup cranks.

"I'm a dirt farmer," Walt Berger said, "too poor to survive and too stubborn to move on. Thor and Agatha Voldheim are neighbors to my Beth and me, they and those Js of theirs: John the oldest, cute little Jane, and Jimmy. We do for ourselves, use what the Lord provides, live off the sour, peaty soil. Being neighbors means more than living alongside; have a problem, ask for help. That's why we were together today.

"Fuel grows all over this land. Trees were here first and maybe it's God's plan they'll be here last. This morning we went out to Thor's back forty, where the birch trees grow. We drove the trat, the old cut-off Model A with a homemade boom welded onto where the back seat used to be. I don't know why 'trat'; just always called it that.

"It was still fall this morning when we started, October-warm, like on Halloween night when John and Jane came to our place, jumping in excitement, a wild pirate and blond witch; couldn't understand how Beth and I knew who they were. You know how warm it's been, fooling willows into growing catkins, drizzly, almost muggy. Then old man north wind called and winter began at 10:15 A.M.

"I did the cutting, have a new Husqvarna, proud of that noisy monster. Tell the truth, I hate to let anyone else use it, so I cut and built a small pile of logs, white-barked with those black diamonds, like the Lord didn't want to overdo the white. Thor used the trat, started out dragging logs, piling them by the barn.

"Farming's hard work and I ain't exactly soft, but when you bend and twist to lop limbs it catches you in the back. I'd set the saw down and straightened up, was sort of rubbing things, when I saw it.

"Thor must have tired of dragging. Every root in the county pokes up through the black muck of such a swampy place, enough to catch a log when you're dragging it. He was carrying one by the middle, dangling from the trat's boom when it snagged on a tree. I guess Thor didn't notice, and he drove on until the boom line pulled straight out behind him.

"I screeched, 'Watch out!' He turned his head just as— Maybe he heard me, or felt its pull. When the log broke free it swung toward him like the pendulum of Dad's old grandpa clock.

"It took him alongside the head, butt first, all those hundreds of pounds of swinging force. I've poleaxed cattle and I've always marveled at how instantly floppy they are. Dear God, Thor, he did the same."

I squeezed Walt's shoulder again and returned to the head

of Thor's bed. I lifted his eyelids, shined a light into them, went to the door of the room and called, "Any word yet?"

"No," said nurse Edna Freeman. "I have a line open to Hollings out at the airport; he's on the radio, waiting."

I explained to Walt. "An ambulance plane is on the way from Duluth, and a neurosurgeon friend from intern days is aboard."

"He's hurt bad, ain't he, Doc?"

"Real bad, Walt. He needs an operation soon if he's to have a chance."

"Any chance? You know how it is, Doc: your friend, you see him nearly every day. You talk and b-s and even argue once in a while. We're young, the both of us, with kids and in debt and still in love with our wives. Then your friend gets hurt. One second, he's the same as always, a working stiff trying to get ahead, sitting there on the trat, thinking about . . . his family? The Vikings football game? Then your friend can't hear you anymore. You call and you run and you holler at him, afraid to touch him but wondering if you should straighten him out.

"And now he's lying there. Doc, I'm scared. Thor could die and Aggie could be a widow."

Overhead a roaring grew until it became louder than the wind. An airplane! Edna called from the phone at the desk. "Hollings says they're circling. He'll drive that Dr. Greenly here—Hello, Hollings? . . . Slow down: you're talking too fast. Oh, Doctor, he says the pilot won't land! Crosswinds, forty-five knots, gusts higher."

Two thousand feet away, and as remote as Siberia. I shoved the phone at Walt. "Bring that to the operating room door; it has a long cord. You must help. Ask Hollings to talk to the surgeon on the radio, then you tell me what he says to do. Edna has to assist me."

"Doc, I can't—"

"Do it, Walt!"

"Yes . . . yes, sir. Hollings? Doc MacDonald wants you to talk to the airplane doc. He's to tell . . . Doc, do you have a . . . a tree finder?"

"Trephine. No, we don't."

"All right, do you have a . . . a brace and bit?! That's what he said, Doc."

"Tell him I have an electric bone drill and bits up to one-quarter inch."

"He says to make an . . . insurgeon? Oh, a cut. In the scalp above the ear . . ."

I felt almost calm at the prospect of doing something. The sides of Thor's head were puffy and blue. I incised the skin and carried the wound down to the bone. The drill whined, boring through the skull with a singed-chicken odor. I grunted. A spurt of dark blood. I went to the other side.

I pulled off my rubber gloves and went to Walt in the doorway, where he clung grimly to the jamb with the hand that wasn't crushing the phone nearly in two. I clapped him on the shoulder. "Thank you, Walt, and so would Thor if he could. Maybe we gave him his chance."

Thor died an hour later.

Double Play

FOLKS IN THE FAR NORTH regularly amazed me with a casual disregard for the laws of physics. Escapades of two friends come to mind.

In the emergency room, I found nurse Edna standing beside a gurney holding Clyde Damian. Clyde farmed west of Northpine: oats, hay, dairy cows. He was ambitious and undaunted by government policy or nature's fickle regard for his efforts.

Clyde Damian let out the "kid" bottled up inside his sober propriety by riding a motorcycle. I don't mean that he was roughrider reckless. It's just that, well, I don't expect to see the church usher roar off perched on his Harley. Motorcycles frighten me. Not that they weren't good for business: the Kincaid youngster, both legs broken, and Seth Palmer, all those abrasions. Of course, Sandy Farmer colors my opinion, decerebrate for so many years before he mercifully died.

Clyde lay flat on the table, hands under his head. He grinned sideways at me and winked at Edna.

"Tell me about this accident," I said. I studied him. Something was different. The same broad smile, a friendly crinkle about the eyes. A scraggly beard was darker than his chestnut hair—a beard? Three days before he had been clean-shaven. I said, "Will someone tell me what this is all about? And when did you sprout whiskers?" I looked at him face-on.

The left half of his face sported inch-long whiskers, but the right half was Clyde-smooth. He cackled.

"I was riding my bike," he said, "coasting along peaceful and serene. It was dark except for a little bit of moon hunkering on the horizon. There was a shadow, like when you think you see something out of the corner of your eye, then whap! I stopped like an egg hitting the floor."

He looked at Edna and they hee-hawed in a thoroughly disgusting way. "Anyway," said Clyde, "I sat up in the road and looked around, gathering my thoughts from where they sprawled in the dirt. My bike lay on its side, muttering at me, blinded, its headlight smashed.

"Then I heard a snort like a leaky bagpipe. Something came between me and the moon. I touched a dang hairy tree trunk. It moved and my eyes arranged themselves so I could see what was there. Doc, I broad-sided a moose! Now, Mr. Moose was figuring things out, too, getting ready to object. I could sort of understand, a Harley-Davidson and me at thirty miles an hour. I scooted backwards fast as a crawdad and set out making amends." Clyde patted the air and made kissy noises. "Nice moose, friendly moose." He touched his hirsute adornment gingerly. "The beard? Moose hairs. I snatched him bald."

After Clyde left, Edna handed me a sign she had made while I was tweezing out all those hollow hairs implanted in his cheek. "You can hang it alongside your shingle," she said.

It read: "MacDonald Depilatory Clinic." That woman had a warped sense of humor.

Then there was my friend, Ben. I finished my examination. "You have a hernia all right. When did you first notice it?"

Benjamin Sagquist jerked tight the belt of his woodsman's

pants and scanned the ceiling in thought. "Last night. Must have been about 7:30? Give, take five minutes."

My eyebrows registered surprise. "I'm not used to such precise information. What happened at 7:30?"

"I was carrying Ferdinand."

"Come again?"

"Jackass. Little horse." He shifted a quid of tobacco to the other cheek and inspected me stolidly.

"Ben, I have the oddest feeling that I'll wish I hadn't asked, but why were you carrying a jackass?"

"I got me a hit, Doc."

I blinked like a daytime owl.

Ben waved his hand impatiently. "Donkey baseball. None them outfield jackasses would go near the ball, but Ferdinand kept a bucking and wouldn't run the dang bases. Made me mad, so I picked him up and walked around them myself. There was a whale of a argument, but we won 'cause they couldn't find no rule saying who had to be carrying what. Dang jackass never did quit bucking; that's how come I strained myself."

Ben looked for a place to spit his tobacco, remembered his manners—and swallowed.

Roxie

W HEN ONE IS an isolated country doctor, friends become
patients, and patients become friends.

Roxie Bascolm was twenty-one years old that chilly day
in April. She managed to look like a child imitating maturity,
with her garish eye shadow, dime-store lashes, and a skirt that
stopped just above her knees (until she sat down). Spiked heels
made her gait unsteady. I laid her spanking-new chart on my
desk and studied her. "Tell me about yourself," I said.

I had to strain to hear her answer: "I don't feel good." I asked
general questions—marital status, living arrangements—to
which she responded that she "wasn't in the family way." When
she wasn't staring at her fists, clenched on her lap, she kept
peeking at me through a fringe of chestnut-colored hair with
eyes of a startlingly blue shade.

Finally I said, "Just tell me what I need to know."

She flicked her hand across her lower abdomen. "I get pains
down there and my monthlies won't quit."

"How long has this been going on?"

She mumbled, "A while." I asked her if she was sexually active, and she said, "Who wants to know?" I explained how
signs of early pregnancy could imitate other conditions and
that I needed to know if it was possible. She said, "I s'pose." She
acknowledged that she "didn't hardly never" use contracep-
tives, described her pain as like a mouse nibbling. As I asked my

questions, she began to open up and respond freely. Then she confided that she had consulted a doctor in a neighboring town, and he had given her a shot of penicillin. When I asked her what he had found through a pelvic exam, she said, "He didn't do one." I handed Roxie a sheet and gown and went for the nurse.

I could not do a pelvic exam on Roxie Bascolm. She removed the necessary clothing and lay back on our examination table without demur, but she clamped her legs together so tightly that it was impossible to perform the procedure. When we again returned to my consultation office, Roxie plopped onto the client's chair, in full retreat behind her bangs. I sat across from her and apologized silently to my colleague with the quick penicillin trigger. I struggled to keep roughness out of my voice when I asked her, "What do you suggest we do now, Miss Bascolm?" Her head tipped forward and I read sullenness. "Do you want me to refer you to someone else?"

The fringe of hair shimmied when she shook her head. There were tears in her voice. "I want you to doctor me."

I handed her a box of tissues and leaned toward her. "Is there something you need to tell me?" Her head jerked up and I saw that cobalt blue, swimming in pools of tears. "Want to tell me? Anything?"

"That sexual active thing, did you mean—do I do it?" I nodded, intent. She said, "I do it, but not with *him* anymore, not with Dad."

"Your—*dad?*"

"It began when I was about six, I think. When do you start school? Him and my two brothers and Fogarty, Mom's brother." I blurted something I'd learned in the locker room, then apologized. She just laughed.

"How long did this go on?" I asked.

She shrugged. "Like, always."

"How often?"

"Several times a week, with one or the other. My monthlies helped."

I stammered, "What about your mother?"

"*Her!* She stays out of the way, but she knows. I told my sister once. She's older'n me. She won't talk to me anymore, says I'm a liar, but I'm not!"

I sat back and a mist filled my eyes. "I wouldn't have believed such a thing was possible."

"It's true."

"I believe you, it's just so foreign to what—I never think to ask, even consider—" I tried to imagine myself in her shoes. "What was it like for you?"

Roxie had swept back her hair and she looked me squarely in the eye. "In the beginning you do it because your dad asks you to, to be good, do what your folks want. When you get older—who wants to have the shit knocked out of them? When I found out other kids didn't have to ... It hurts sometimes ... I tried to kill myself once. I bought a new dress when I was sixteen, charged it to Dad. He pounded on me when he found out. I knew he'd pay for it if I let him have sex—he always did—but I just didn't want to.

"Mom uses pills all the time: sleeping pills, nerve pills, pep pills. I took all of them I could find. They hauled me into a hospital and pumped my stomach, but I was out for two days."

"What did your doctor say when you told him?"

"Doctors don't want to hear stuff like that. Oh, I wonder why I told you. Maybe 'cause you don't act like a doctor. Oh my gosh."

"That's the nicest compliment I've had in a month," I said.

"Does you father still bother you?" She said that he tried. "How you must feel toward him."

"I love him; we're very close. 'Course, I won't see him alone, just when someone else is around." When I sputtered, she said, "A person needs a father. I just do it with boys now, not *him* or my brothers. Or Fogarty. He's the worst. Do you want to examine me?"

I went for nurse Elaine Andresen.

Roxie and I returned to my consultation office for the third time that afternoon and sat facing each other. Doctors must preserve the professional façade. Feelings are for patients, or private times at best. I strove mightily, and failed. My voice was its own master. I croaked out something.

Roxie's pelvis was a mass of cancer, stony-hard, ravening. Her internal female organs were no longer recognizable as such.

My friend Roxie died just before Christmas.

Coroner

"UNDER OLD ENGLISH LAW, you would be the only person empowered to arrest the sheriff," said county attorney Elwin Morris.

"Why would I want to do that?" I asked.

Sam Hargrave, my friend and colleague from neighboring Koochiching, wiggled his eyebrows. "Don't be evasive, RAM," he said. "We all agreed that we need a medical person as county coroner. We'll help finance your campaign."

"I know nothing about the job. What would I have to do?"

Elwin Morris said, "Investigate unattended deaths, accidents, homicides, suicides. Hold inquests when appropriate. As county attorney, I'll help you with the legal procedures. Obviously you can handle the medical aspects far better than the layman who is our present coroner. Every certificate he has signed for the past decade gave as cause of death 'acute stoppage of the heart.'"

"But—campaign? Holy buckets."

Elwin smiled confidently. "Just file, then community common sense will prevail. You'll be elected."

"My wife isn't keen on this." Sam Hargrave said something about civic duty. "Well . . ."

The number of hats a doctor must wear is proportional to his distance from a large city. I was elected county coroner on November 2, 1954. My tour of duty began January 1. Steve Kinney was my first case.

Trevor Baldridge of the U.S. Air Force was a lad from Alabama. He had been ordered to the Sioux Lookout Air Base in northwestern Ontario, Canada. He traveled north that January day along the U.S. highway that was Northpine's link with the rest of Minnesota. Snow pelted his car. He did not understand that a swirling, moving whiteout ahead meant that he followed a loaded pulpwood truck. Confused, he drove cautiously down the middle of the road. Steve Kinney was coming from the opposite direction. They collided head-on, just behind the truck, in that moment of snowy blindness when driving depends on faith in one's fellows.

Steve was a fine young man.

Violent death, with its gore and disruption of form, the eager putrefaction when death is not discovered promptly, allowing nature's cleanup crew of bacteria, flies, and maggots to intervene—such cases were difficult for me. The job could be hard work physically; deputy sheriff Roger Edwards and I carried Swan Nelson out of the woods through heavy snow when a tree fell on his head. Another time Rog and I pulled out a "floater," six months lost in the river, dragging the man's body up those steep, mucky, black-clay banks with a rope. Rog did not retain his breakfast and I was glad I had not had time to eat.

For a coroner, 100% of cases are "bad outcomes." I wondered if emotional calluses were possible.

Rarely in my life have I fired a gun. I have no serious quarrel with those who hunt, but being a coroner quickly taught me respect for guns. As a rural physician, I regularly dealt with wounds caused by firearms, near-miss threats to life: Nils Tversdahl, who lost a leg when a "stray" rifle bullet severed the main artery in his thigh, or bird hunter Evan Simon, who rested the barrel of his .410 shotgun atop his foot and absent-mindedly pulled the trigger.

A coroner, on the other hand, mops up after shots that do not miss. Consider the case of Matt Shapchuk:

Age forty-three. Paper maker at the mill in Koochiching. Divorced. Matt lived alone. A fellow worker investigated when he failed to show up for his shift and found him dead in bed. Deputy sheriff Roger Edwards, city officer Andy Botsford, and I met at Matt's house.

The man lay on his left side, facing an outside wall. He wore undershorts, to all appearances peacefully asleep. Blood drenched the mattress from a jagged wound in the front of his chest, directly over the heart. I found a lump beneath the skin of his back, a slug, battered and misshapen. The pellet had been fired from a rifle. We found no weapon. There was no room between the wall and the front of Matt's chest to place a rifle; we could not reconstruct the shooting. After we removed Matt's body, Deputy Edwards and I returned to the cabin. Frustrated, I knelt beside the bed. The day was November-gray, late in the afternoon by this time. Kneeling, I saw a tiny spot of light at eye level, a hole in the wall of the house. We scrambled outdoors.

Matt Shapchuk lived in the last place on the edge of town. A small garden stood open between it and the forest. Even as we watched, a deer tiptoed cautiously into the field and pawed at a crust of snow. Deer hunting season. A mushrooming bullet fired from a deer rifle. A man shot dead in his home by an unknown hunter, unknowing. A remarkable event born of ironic coincidence, never to be repeated.

Until six weeks later. Jamison Anders worked for Butch Tyson in a logging camp forty miles southwest of Northpine. He was target shooting with a .22 pistol and a stray shot pierced the wall of Fred Diggerbang's shack. By coincidence, Fred was napping on his cot. The bullet went unerringly through his heart. Fred appeared to be sleeping on his side when we arrived.

Coincidence

FEBRUARY IN NORTHPINE is the most predictable month of the year. Cold, such a stark word, is monarch. Cold. Skin freezes in seconds and delicate lungs ache in dread of the next breath. Snow underfoot creaks, crunches, snaps. A cannon boom reverberates through the total stillness of a fifty-below night in the forest, the death lament of a great frozen tree when it splits apart. Cold is the lingering, harmonic, metallic ringing produced when two ordinary icicles are struck together at forty-five below. It is the banshee howling of rapidly freezing ice, its contraction goading a lake into protest, so oddly and uniquely harmonious.

Cold complicated human vanity that February of 1950.

It was the evening of February 22, Washington's birthday. The air was still, the thermometer at twenty-seven degrees below zero. A full moon reflected off clean billows of snow, providing enough light for one gifted with sharp eyesight to read by it.

Sven Anderson and his wife, Betty, both twenty-three, together with a young neighbor spent a quiet, sociable evening at a tavern. Sven was a responsible citizen who sipped two beers to make them last. They left at 10:05 P.M. and climbed into the cab of the pulpwood-truck tractor Sven used to haul wood every day. An electrical short caused all the lights to go out. Already weary, planning to get up at 4:00 the next morning, Sven had no patience with trying to fix it that night.

Paul Barg offered to take them home. He reported to me later that his friend decided the moon was so bright he could see the road well enough to drive the five miles home. Paul watched him leave, steering by the painted centerline, which was faintly luminous in the silver light.

Patients are always afraid, or hurting, or both. My well-developed bump of empathy often forced me to journey for a while in the footsteps of those who sought my help. In my mind I rode with the Andersons that night. Did they laugh and joke, nervous about their unusual circumstances? They met one car on a perfectly straight stretch of highway. Sven pulled over until it passed before starting up again at a cautious thirty-five miles an hour. They neared home; did they sigh with relief?

When they died it was like swatted flies, for the motor of the old Mack truck slammed completely inside the cab against the seat on which they sat. No lebensraum, no living-breathing-heart-beating space was left to them. Radiator to radiator, they had crashed into a pulp-truck tractor driven by Ted Samuelson, coming from the opposite direction at a cautious thirty-five miles an hour. A truck with no lights.

Ted had found his truck lights inoperable that cold but so-brilliantly-moonlit evening. He had set out, knowing he had only three miles to go, relying on the brightness of the night. His truck was larger and newer than Sven's, and its motor stopped two feet short of the back of its crumpled cab. All four Samuelsons survived the crash. Caught in the remnants of their steel mousetrap, however, his daughter and grandson did not escape the cold, for sundered metal is no protection against such temperatures. Late-evening travel in that land of hard-working people was limited. The next motorists to pass by did not do so for nearly an hour.

Ted's wife survived near demolition of her foot and ankle. He was almost unhurt, physically. There remained the problem of nightmares.

Did either driver have a premonition? Did either catch a last microsecond glint of moonlight from an oncoming windshield before their panes came to rest two feet apart? Ted cannot remember, and I had no chance to ask Sven.

Cops and Robbers

MEDICAL EDUCATION NEVER CEASES. Doctors attend seminars where lecturers present topics dear to their hearts. More often than not, they are useful. The problem, of course, is that a patient does not hear the same lectures and may choose to present herself in a thoroughly confusing manner. Consider children's medicine. When it comes to practical pediatrics, nothing comes close to having kids of your own. If a distraught mother told me that her daughter would not take the medicine I had prescribed, my thought was, "Lady, who's in charge?" Such judgmental complacency did not last through my daughter Mary's first year of life.

A child's job is to test her boundaries, a parent's to see that she survives the tests. The thing about parenting is that there are never days off.

I picked a chart from the holder beside Room Two of my Northpine office. Nurse Elaine Andresen had pinned a note to the front of it: "gunshot wound." My pulse leaped.

Inside the crowded exam room I found Dickie Sanford, age nine, his cheeks damp with tears; Garner, age ten; Florenda, their mother, looking as though she had just emerged from a hotly contested rummage sale; and Peter, the boys' father. He stood in the far corner, looking grim.

Dickie clung to his mother. He wiped his nose on a frayed

sleeve and returned my inspection apprehensively. I lifted him onto the end of the exam table. Alert, not obviously bleeding or in agony. "Where did you get hit?" I asked.

Florenda waved her hand like a child claiming the teacher's attention. "Wait!"

All my experience with Florenda had taught me to keep a tight rein on her considerable volubility. "I'd like to get the story from Dickie," I said firmly. I glanced at his father, Peter, seeking reinforcement. He stood in the corner, looking grim.

I turned back to Dickie. He lifted a hip and patted his buttock. "Oh my, shot in the butt? With what?"

Florenda's hand was now waving inches before my nose. "A shotgun, but—"

I ostentatiously turned a shoulder toward her. "Let's get a look at the damage."

He undid his britches. Smooth, white, little-boy buttocks. No blood. I said, "I don't see—"

"Got a larruping from Ma."

"She spanked you for getting shot?"

Florenda shouted into my ear, "Garner's the one got shot. Dickie had the gun."

The quintessential art of diagnosis is a willingness to change one's mind when further evidence points away from an original conclusion. I may have blushed, though.

I gingerly asked Master Garner if and where he might have been shot. He touched the front of his chest. After peeling off his shirt, I studied the lad. A single drop of blood, directly over the sternum.

"Someone tell me what happened."

Peter looked at the ceiling, grim. Florenda turned her waggling finger onto Garner. "Tell him!"

"We uns was playing—"

"All six kids home 'cause of mud vacation," Florenda shrilled. "How can they not have school?"

"You was playing," I urged Garner.

"Sorta cops an' robbers, an' I got to be the robber an' Dickie, he had the gun—"

"Our twelve gauge," Florenda said.

"—an' I held up the bank an' was makin' my getaway, an' Dickie, he shot at me—"

"With the *twelve* gauge," Florenda said.

"—an' I kinda ducked behind a tree, but it stung me."

I sidled past Peter, standing in the corner, looking grim, and made out requisitions for a series of chest x-rays.

There was a shotgun pellet directly in the center of Garner's chest. Except for the evidence on film, I would have concluded the boy was unharmed. Not sure what else to do, I admitted him to the hospital.

I examined Garner the next morning. No fever, no signs of infection, lungs clear and unaffected, his heart unconcerned. On some peculiar whim I ordered another chest x-ray.

The pellet had vanished.

I retrieved the films from the day before. Dense foreign body, lead pellet. Today, nothing.

I worked through the morning, but the mystery of the disappearing pellet constantly intruded. At noon I returned to scan the films again. Where could the darn thing have gone? I noticed something at the very bottom edge of the film and ordered another x-ray.

In the right lower quadrant of Garner's abdomen was the x-ray shadow of a single lead pellet. Reconstruction: it had penetrated the boy's sternum, pierced the front wall of the esophagus, been cast into the stream of his digestive tract, and nature was handling it the same as it would anything else bold enough to enter the alimentary system.

I sent Garner home the following morning. He was loath to leave, not being accustomed to having ice cream three times a day. Florenda was quiet, save for a toss of the chin and a snort she aimed in my direction. She marched down the hall to the exit, a firm hold on Garner's ear.

I turned to Peter. "Your wife didn't have much to say today." He broke into a stubble-cheeked grin. "Nope."

Inheritance

A s I drove past the sign that confirmed the existence of Northpine, Minnesota, I fought to stay awake. It was midnight-dark on a cloudy, moonless night in April, black everywhere save the ribbon of gravel road revealed under the probing of my headlights. Then full wakefulness took command. Ahead, an orange puffball of light grew, restless, writhing. Goaded by adrenaline, I speeded up.

What did I know about Jacob Hankinson? Sixtyish. Widower. Farmer of sorts, at least by northern Minnesota definition. Occasional patient. Reclusive. Stoic. I sped south toward the balloon of lurid radiance.

Jake's wife, Alvina, had died at age fifty, soon after my arrival in town, her life shortened by unrelenting work. Were there kids? Deputy sheriff Roger Edwards would know.

Fire now dominated the sky. Sparks and embers soared into the air to join a roiling cloud of smoke lit from below. I parked behind a row of cars, found myself running lemming-like, stumbling over ruts, pulse pounding and breathless.

Jacob Hankinson's house was a large frame two-and-a-half-story building, replica of so many farmhouses that dot rural America. Built to house families in an era when farm prosperity lay in proportion to the number of strong sons available, such dwellings were hopeful wooden castles.

Roger Edwards's familiar bulk detached itself from a throng of blank-faced figures. "Quite a sight," he said.

Jets of flame shot from every aperture of the old building, roaring, devouring spouts of fire. Behind the house, burning with equal gusto, stood the barn, rapidly disappearing. To one side a shed of some kind conducted its own immolation rites, and a garage yawned as a square of fire. Inside it huddled a pickup truck, outlined in smoky orange, a dark negative image. Its gas tank exploded, and the structure became a brief flame-thrower. A great tree near the house flared, a sudden torch. As one the crowd stepped back a pace. I wrinkled my nose. Scorched wood, burning paint and shingles. I looked again at the barn. Charred flesh. The still night pressed around, windless except for the draft spawned by the fire itself.

I shivered. "Rog, is Jake in there?"

Deputy Edwards shrugged. "No one has seen him, so probably yes. The fire is obviously incendiary. The neighbors who reported it said everything was burning at once."

"Fill me in on what you know about Jake," I said.

"His dad was a homesteader up here. Logging companies scalped the land and moved on, but guys like Ansel Hankinson stayed behind and tried to farm. Swamp, sandy ridges, rocks everywhere, pretty tough. Jake took over the place after Ansel died. The tradition, work the land and keep it in the family. He and Alvina had . . . let's see, Vera, Minnie, and . . . oh yes, Alice. Three girls in pretty much a hurry, but no sons. That must have soured Jake: all those females, no boy to teach desperation farming to. He kept more and more to himself, never a cheery word, even nasty.

"A few years later, Alvina found herself with child again, finally had them a boy. All of a sudden Jake found meaning in life again. Those three daughters of his were fine gals—I had a crush on Vera in high school—but Jake didn't seem to value them. Jacob Junior, now . . .

"Jake started pounding hardscrabble farming into that boy's head from the time he could raise it up and look around. You can guess how Jake the younger came to regard such a way of life. He escaped to the U. S. of A. army soon as he could convince the recruiter he was old enough. It was from the safety of a foxhole in Korea that the boy wrote his pa and told him in plain terms that he wasn't going to continue the family tradition of the land."

Rog shook his head sheepishly. "Doc, I'm seeing that I got you here too soon. We'll have to let it burn out, find what we can come daylight."

Dawn tinted the sky gray when my phone rang again. Roger said, "I found Jake."

The deputy stood beside the acrid, smoking basement. He gave me a tired, two-fingered salute and kicked a char into the black hole before him. He started toward a pasture behind the barn, two or three acres of fenced-in brown grass stippled with green shoots, bold adventurers into the frosty air. A sun caught between red and gold melted away clouds and promised to free puddles from their skims of ice. Frost covered the ground, a mantle speckled with minute jewels in homage to the sun.

Roger led me past the burned-out barn. Near the back of the pasture was a piled row of rocks, legacy of some glacier, a cairn. We walked toward them and what they held. I trudged across frozen grass that whispered underfoot, my breath coming in rasps.

Jake's body sprawled across the rock pile. His skull was cleaved raggedly. I forced myself to inspect (the clinical attitude), to visualize (the rifle barrel in his mouth; pull the trigger with a thumb), to empathize (the culmination of a life). Against all volition I shuddered. Roger croaked, "Me too. All his stock was in the barn. Unless I miss my guess, he'd shot them first. I hope."

"Do you suppose he was watching all of us before?"

"I've been here the rest of the night; I'd have heard the gun. When? I suppose once he got it going good, maybe when he heard the first car coming. He was determined that his kids would get nothing but this." Roger glanced around the fields of sour, thin soil. He nudged the rifle with his toe. "And this."

Frank Petruka

FRANK PETRUKA was job foreman for a company that harvested Christmas trees. Roads through much of the vast northern wilderness were crude and transient. Frank and one of his men, Lars Oddem, set out that bleak November day in a heavy-duty company pickup truck, leaving Frank's personal car at Loading Station Nine. They carried dynamite, caps, fuse, and an assortment of hand tools.

The truck crawled over ridges of frozen mud and small drifts of winter's first snow to the section of road where they would be working. The land cleared of timber, only stumps remained, barriers daunting as tank traps. The men were experienced and worked well as a team: dig a hole, place a charge under a stump, tamp sand and dirt carefully, light the fuse, and trot to one side. They loosened half a dozen stumps and moved on to the next.

"Coffee time?" Lars asked.

Frank grunted. "After this one. Pack it good, now." The fuse hissed and they ran toward the truck. They waited. A raven cawed, raucous and indignant. A whiskey jack landed on the remnant of a small balsam tree and eyed them quizzically. Frank glanced at his watch. "How long a fuse did you use, Lars?"

"Same as always. Thirty seconds or so."

"It's been a minute and a half," Frank said.

Lars kicked a clod of ice. "Give it another minute."

The two men circled the stump like dogs sizing up rivals. No smoke, no hiss. They stared at the filled tamp hole. A pungency, burnt fuse powder. Frank muttered and stretched out his left hand.

When the dynamite exploded, it blew sand and gravel into Lars's face and he was blinded on the instant. Frank now had only one hand. Instinctively he used it to cradle the shredded mess of bone, muscle, and skin that had been his other hand and forearm. The left side of his face wept bits of tissue and blood but no tears, for the eye no longer existed.

Lars had two hands but could not see. Frank had the use of his right eye but only one hand. The pickup was powerful but awkward to drive.

Frank led Lars to the driver's seat. He told him what to do: "Back up, Lars. Stop. Shift forward, pull left . . . left! You almost—Right, now . . . careful . . . There's a rock big as a piano . . ."

They drove the two miles to Loading Station Nine with a blind man at the wheel. There they transferred to Frank's car with its automatic shift.

The car slid off the scraggly road. Frank clutched the steering wheel. "Get out and push, Lars."

"I can't—God, Frank, my eyes."

Frank said, "Slide over and take the wheel." He crawled out and leaned against the car. He worked his way to the back and planted his feet in snow. "Rock it, Lars!" He groaned when he pushed with his shoulder and left bloody prints of his right hand all over the trunk. Drive wheels whined when they spun on snow but Frank refused to quit. The car crept forward, back onto the road. "Stop!" he shouted. He floundered through the snow. "Move over, I'll drive again."

They arrived at base camp. Men with gnarled hands, fellow workers, lifted them gently out of the car.

I sent Lars to Duluth to see an eye specialist. As for Frank, I spent the afternoon cleaning, trimming, salvaging what was possible. A stump just below the elbow. A face half-and-half. One clear eye.

Lars's eyes healed well enough that he returned to work in the woods. His corneas were scarred; he told me that a bright day was like a Lake Superior fog. He shrugged. "That's life, Doc."

And Frank? He never lost a sturdy determination. He said, "Way I see it, Doc, life with one hand's a sight better'n life with none."

May Day, May Day

THE CALLAHANS. Although Rich was from Newark, New Jersey, he was more fiercely Irish than most who had trod the emerald sward all their lives. When it came to skills to gladden the heart of a truly isolated rural physician, Rich had no peer. Lab, x-ray, scrub to help in surgery—name it.

Wife Margery Callahan was a Swedish farm girl from western Minnesota who had mastered the art of living serenely with the volatility of a Celtic temperament. She and Rich were a happy couple. Additionally, Margery was a fabulous medical stenographer. My wife used to complain that I spent more time talking to Marg than I did to her, via the electronic chains of dictating equipment. Barb was kidding. I think.

The Callahans joined us there in Northpine during the summer of 1956. That fall and early winter, mayhem took up housekeeping in our town.

Greg Nolan jacked up his tractor, fastened a power take-off to one rear wheel, ran a belt to a great circular saw, and prepared to cut firewood. He caught a hand in the belt and jerked off his arm just below the elbow.

Ozzie Teichman drove his pulp truck into the side of a Northern Pacific locomotive. This did the train little harm, but Ozzie rearranged sundry parts of his anatomy. What concerned him was his truck. "Only half paid-for, Doc, and that sucker is, I mean, totaled."

Fritz Opper, on the other hand, reversed the order of things. A Duluth, Mesabi and Iron Range diesel smacked him over in Norsk Township. Joe Feras saw the whole affair and told me, "The only t'ing went higher up in the air than all them pulp sticks was old Fritz hisself, only they didn't say nothin', but you could hear Fritz going up *and* coming down. It was beaut'ful— such words I never heard before."

A boy down at Long Rapids got up early one morning and wandered out to the back pasture on his parents' farm. Todd was twelve, an avid hunter, a student because he had no choice. The school bus came and went before his mother realized Todd had not returned to the house. She found him lying on the ground, his beloved .22 rifle at his side. The hole in his temple wasn't enormous, just large enough.

Left-over lumberjack Lars Forston lived in the battered relic of what had been a hotel during the heyday of the defunct logging town of Craig's Landing. As was his wont, he took a bottle of whiskey to bed with him one night. In alcoholic befuddlement, he stepped through the second-story window of his room on the way to the biffy. Crushed both heel bones.

Nils Yeager caught his right hand in the whirling blade of a large circular platform saw. He arrived at the emergency room with only one digit still present, the ring finger. Its flexor tendon was gone, but I was able to connect the tendon from the missing index finger to it. Six months later, Nils wiggled his one-fingered hand at me and said, "It works, Doc, as long as I remember to think it's my *first* finger."

The highway department embarked on a bridge-maintenance program. Sid Long fell from a span and landed on his head.

I said to Sid in the emergency room, "How are you?"

"Not too bad, Doc. Got a little headache, right there." He pointed at the top of his head. A great jagged crescent ran across his pate. Blood soaked his hair, blood and something white and cheesy. I lifted the flap of skin and a section of bone the size of my hand came with it. I was peering deep into the man's head. Cheesy-white something—brain matter!

I said, "You are—"

"In a hurry, Doc," he interrupted. "Slap a couple of stitches in that and let me get back to work. We have to finish tomorrow."

I replaced the flap, resisting an impulse to pat it into place. A divot. "Sid," I said, "you need far more than—"

"Doc, don't make a federal case of this."

The man survived. So far as any of us could tell, he didn't miss the portion of his brain that ended up in the shampoo rinse.

Then there was Alvin. You know how some people always leap before they look? Alvin was helping his brother Holden top off a stack of hay, slid down off it when they had finished, and landed squarely on the upturned tines of a three-prong hayfork, sending it into his chest. To the hilt.

Holden brought him to the emergency room. It was hard to say which brother looked the more frazzled. Holden explained what had happened. I asked, "Then who—Someone must have pulled out the fork."

Holden said, "Oh, I had to do that, 'counta we couldn't get Alvin in the dang car, the handle sticking out so dang far."

The tines missed Alvin's heart but collapsed one lung. He cussed all the way to Duluth, then wouldn't let the doctor down there put him in the hospital.

Cussed some on the way back, too, so I heard.

There is a ski hill near Northpine. Over the course of time, I became acquainted with many a participant in the sport. (I once totaled up the number of leg fractures I had set: came to well above the five hundred mark.)

During the season, Saturday was ski-fracture day. Sometimes gurneys would be lined up in the hallway outside the procedure room, waiting. This was particularly true when a prestigious college in southern Minnesota sent a busload or two of young people to the resort for a week of skiing. I never understood what there was about that particular brand of us Lutherans.

A lad had broken his tibia and fibula, a routine ski fracture. I finished my usual non-operative approach to the injury, capturing a satisfactory position of the broken bones in plaster. When I ducked into the hall to see who else was waiting, nurse Edna Freeman caught my scrub-suit tails.

"You have a phone call," she said, "from Washington, D.C."

Now, the president never consults me, although if he would I'd be glad to give him an earful, so I was intrigued.

"From the state department," she said. Her eyes were round as coins.

I picked up the receiver and cleared my throat. "Uh—Hello?"

The voice was silky with diplomatic finesse. "I'm told you have [voice pronounced the name I had been trying to decipher from the youth's chart] and we at state are wondering what you have *done* with him."

I explained: broken leg, in a cast, resting comfortably.

"You are an orthopedic surgeon? Doctor?"

"Orthopedics anyway. The boy needed no operation."

"I'm sure you understand, Doctor, what our concerns are."

"Actually, no. I kind of wondered, in fact."

"But surely, even in—let's see. Minnesota? Yes, out west somewhere. You must be aware of the implications. Our national interests. Stability in the region. Ambassadorship."

"Sir, I haven't been this confused all month. Who is this fellow?"

"You didn't know his name?!"

"It's on his record, and he's with a bunch of students from [that Lutheran college]. Although, I'm not certain he's a Lutheran."

"Sir! He is the son of [voice named the boss of one of those Arabian emirates where turmoil seems to be emblazoned on their crest of arms]. What have you to say?"

"Well, I'm glad I didn't know he wasn't just another Lutheran boy from southern Minnesota *before* I set his fracture. And for whatever it's worth, diplomacy-wise, he seems like a decent kid. Sir."

I'm not sure the voice was placated, but we had no further discourse. I've wondered: Is my name now locked into one of those F.B.I. files you hear about?

I had played on the local softball team with Mike Quist. Nice guy. He had a pair of boys who must surely have been copies of their daddy. Lively. The kids and Betty, his wife, stayed at Mike's logging camp that summer. Young Gar did something with the controls of a parked D-4 Caterpillar dozer, allowing it to ease forward and pin his brother Ralphy across the belly in a mighty metal Heimlich maneuver that ruptured a zillion capillaries.

The lad looked as though someone had dipped his upper half in grape juice. Deep purple. But Ralphy did just fine, after purple went through shades of green and yellow.

And so it went. Rich Callahan was moved to ask me, "Does anyone around here ever die of natural causes?"

Help

ONE EVENING IN 1957 I flopped onto the couch in our
living room.

"I find it hard to believe," I said, "that I once worried about
not having enough to do."

Barbara looked up from her book. "Are you home for good?"

"If I have anything to say about it."

"You have."

A sword turned in a familiar and festering wound. "Not tonight, Barbara, no lecturing, no guilting. I can't help being eter-
nally on call."

"On call! When everyone else in the world is more important than family."

"I'm trying to find a partner! I've written letters, telephoned
people who hung up on me, offered more than we have to give,
but no takers."

"You said this new dean of the medical school, this Dr. Arnold Smith, was a friend."

"Well, friend. He attended on one service while I was a student."

"Don't friends try to help each other? See him, tell him how
badly you need an associate. Isn't the medical school there to
provide doctors for our state?"

"My alma mater has little interest in the problems of rural Minnesota. Besides, Dr. Smith wouldn't know me from the janitor."

"Were you lying, this friendship thing?"

"He just never hollered at me or ridiculed me in front of my comrades. In the one-upmanship hierarchy of a medical school, that's friendly."

"Move away from here."

"Move—What?"

Barbara snatched a tissue from a box on the table at her elbow. "You asked for alternatives to your working all the time. We agreed that a partner was the best answer. Now you tell me none are available. So, move away."

"We can't do that!"

"Why not?"

"These people need us."

"So?"

"You could just walk away?"

"Yes! Maybe. . . . That's not fair. What about us? What's so terrible about wanting a life outside the hospital?"

"I don't know how much good it would do to go down to the medical school." I squirmed under the challenge in Barbara's eyes. "But I'll try."

I arrived at the office of Dr. Arnold Smith on the tick of the hour. First I encountered his secretary, a female dragon we medical students had dubbed Dean Fran (in polite society), on the theory that her iron will was the real power behind this particular throne. She agreed that I had an appointment—she'd made it herself—but it seemed I'd been pre-empted.

"The Dean is *far* too busy with Important Issues to honor your appointment. I'm sure you understand, *Doctor*." She gave "Doctor" that same scornful emphasis I remembered so well, in a tone of voice capable of shriveling a medical student at fifty paces.

"I came nearly three hundred miles for this meeting," I said. "I consider providing physicians for the citizens of our state to be a reasonable activity for this medical school to be involved in. I intend to keep our appointment, thank you."

Dean Fran suggested that I blow it out my ear, not quite that politely. I stormed out of the office and slammed the door hard enough to threaten its opaque glass window, something I'd wanted to do all those years ago. Then I headed for the john. While I stood there communing with that long, white receptacle, coloring the air purple, who should saunter in but Dean Smith himself.

I looked at him sidewise, the way you do in situations like that, and said, "Just the person I had an appointment to meet with."

He blinked and raised his head. "Ah—yes?"

"Ah yes, indeed, sir."

"What about, uh—"

It was clear that my face was dependably forgettable. "Roger MacDonald, graduating class of '46."

Conditions did not invite the custom of shaking hands, but I gained the impression that he would not be unwilling under more propitious circumstances.

I said, "Our appointment was to discuss the acute, even dangerous, shortage of rural physicians." We moved to the washbasins and splashed soap and water merrily. "And the fact that I'm going crazy from overwork in Northpine."

"Where?"

"Up north. Minnesota? I wrote you three times during the past year but received no answer."

"The mail is unreliable these days."

Dean Smith edged toward the door, his scholarly hands now

quite dry. I followed him into the hallway, walking right alongside him as though we were colleagues, buddies even.

"I need help and I want to know what our university, my school, can do. *Will* do. We out there need partners—Excuse me, sir, before you return to your office—Sir?"

His door snicked shut on the fanciest footwork I've seen outside a chorus line. I jerked it open, endured Dean Fran's grade-A scowl for as long as past conditioning would allow, then slammed it with a glorious rattle.

Thank God deans have kidneys! Otherwise we never would have found time to chat.

Is There a Limit?

BARBARA AND I had been to Duluth for the day. We were tired, hoping not too many problems awaited us at home. We rounded a bend in the road and ahead of us the night was filled with garish, flashing red lights. A brief line-up of vehicles threaded through debris from two fragmented cars. My heart pounded.

Officer Curt Innes waved us through the obstacle course. He recognized me and shouted, "Hurry, Doc, they need you at the hospital. Don't spare the gas."

There is a special tension when I speed toward the hospital and serious injury. How many? What catastrophe? It is a time when the young are equally at risk with the old or sick, the body so frail. Please, God, make me equal to the task.

Some friends, a family of Dad, Mom, and three beautiful children, had gone for a ride that evening. They owned a little foreign car. A big station wagon approached them at eighty or ninety miles an hour. It roared up behind another car and the driver must have decided he had time to pass. He darted around it just as my friends arrived and hit them head-on. George, the dad, was killed on the spot. The three kids, between the ages of six and ten, rattled around like popcorn. Somehow Ruth, George's wife, ended up with only a broken arm, mid-radius and ulna. All three children were deeply comatose with eye signs indicating severe brain damage and Cheyne-Stokes periodic respiration, with its terrifying interludes when breathing stops for up to thirty seconds, another sign of severe brain injury.

Cam was the oldest. She had completely quit breathing on her own. Our master of all paramedical skills, Rich Callahan, had already placed a tube into her windpipe and was breathing for her with the gas machine. Every time he stopped, she did. Her pupils were widely dilated, her heart barely plugging along, her limbs fractured, floppy in places nature never put joints.

I readied the other two youngsters for an ambulance trip to Duluth, 165 miles away, hoping to give them a shot. Then I went back to the emergency room and Cam.

To every physician there comes a time when he must say "cease the struggle." It is hard enough to say if the person is an old man fighting his last battle. When it is a beautiful Cam, for a blinding instant I see one of my own daughters, a Mary, a Pam, a Jane, lying on the gurney.

I had already told Ruth about George. Now I had to tell her about Cam. She lay there in bed with big, hurting eyes, watching me. She just said, "Thanks, Doc." I spent the next hour checking her out, splinting her broken arm.

Andy, the ambulance driver, stopped halfway to Duluth to let me know that John had died but that they were going on with Tim, the last of Ruth's children. I had to return and tell her about Johnnie. The same thing: she looked at me with those eyes so full of pain, thanked me.

I went to the doctors' lounge and lay down, wrung out. The night nurse came and told me that Andy had called from St. Luke's Hospital in Duluth. Tim had died just as they reached the hill above Duluth. I made the trip back to Ruth's room, so distraught I could not say one word, just stood there with tears streaming down my face.

She sighed. "Tim died, too."

I pulled up a chair beside her, laid my head on the edge of the bed, and sobbed. She patted me on the head.

I returned to the doctors' lounge and flopped onto the bed. I dropped off into some crazy kind of sleep, then awoke screaming. I scared the poor nurses out from under their caps.

I didn't try to sleep any more that night.

The occupants of the other car were two young men who had bragged to a gas station attendant in Northpine that they would reach the Iron Range, one hundred miles away, in an hour. They received minor injuries but must have decided they wouldn't be very popular in our town, so they insisted on being taken to a hospital in the opposite direction.

As coroner, I conducted an inquest. Officer Curt Innes testified that he had found a pulverized beer bottle between the driver's legs when they pried him out of the car. A timid county attorney charged them with reckless driving. They were ultimately fined $200. That made George and the kids worth $50 apiece.

Consultation

I LUBRICATED THE OUTSIDE of a twenty-centimeter-long proctoscope and said to nurse Edna Freeman, "You can turn off the room light now." I adjusted the spotlight and eased the instrument into place. "Sorry, Ole, but I warned you."

From his head-down position, Ole Munson volunteered his opinion of the process in forthright woodsman's talk. I was embarked on one of the less enjoyable tests a patient must undergo. Too bad it's so important.

Angry red bowel lining slid into view at fifteen centimeters. The inflammatory disease extended to the field limits of the proctoscope, covering all visible surfaces, and was fragile, attested to by many points of fresh, bloody ooze.

Crohn's disease or ulcerative colitis? Perhaps some acute infection. I chewed my lip indecisively, feeling a familiar frustration at being reminded of the limits to my knowledge. For the thousandth time I wished consultations were more readily available. I sighed in resignation and carefully withdrew the scope. "I'll arrange to have a specialist see you, Ole, a proctologist."

After Edna had restored him to a simple kneeling position, Ole asked, "When, Doc?"

"I'll get right on it," I said from the door of the treatment room. I glanced at my old enemy, the clock, swore under my breath, and plunged into the hallway only to carom off a broad masculine abdomen. We exchanged apologies and the casually dressed stranger held out his hand.

"You are Doctor—?"

"MacDonald."

"Glad to meet you. I hope you don't mind if I look around your nice little hospital. Oh, I'm Dr. John Foster of Miami, Florida, up here on a vacation. Back home I'm a proctologist—"

I grabbed his arm. "Doctor, you just went back to work." I ushered him into the treatment room. "I have a patient in here. Ole, meet Dr. Foster, a proctologist. He has agreed to examine you."

Ole's eyes bulged and he let go of his biblike examination gown. "Gawd, Doc, when you say you'll get right on it, you don't fart around."

Bryan Lofgren

B RING TOGETHER A BUNCH OF DOCTORS and try to keep them from talking shop. Ask any physician's spouse: it cannot be done. A certain amount of useful information passes around the profession because of this habit, but, truth to tell, it is bragging rights that fuel most of these confabs. The most unexpected diagnosis? That "fascinoma" not seen since medical-school days? An unusual string of related cases? The most courageous patient ever treated? There I win hands down, because I knew Bryan Lofgren.

He was twenty-three that chilly November day. I had been out in the woods on a coroner case, that of a deer hunter who had dropped of a heart attack. Tramping through snowy brush, helping deputy sheriff Roger Edwards and the man's hunting companion carry out his body, my thoughts were on a warm shower and a quick nap on the couch before supper.

Nurse Edna Freeman was stationed at the hospital door when I returned.

"Hurry, Doctor, in here."

I trotted into the emergency room. Bryan occupied the examination table, curly-headed and solemn. Saline poured through a needle placed in an arm vein. Lab technician Rich Callahan held up a pint of fresh blood. "I have two units ready, two more in the lab. Say the word."

I cocked an eyebrow at Rich. "What—?"

"Gunshot. Belly."

Oh, God.

I stepped alongside the cart. Bryan said, "Glad to see you, Doc."

The Doctor Question, automatically: "How are you?"

"Just fine."

He's talking: mark that as a plus. "What happened?" While he told me, I lifted off the sterile dressings Edna had placed across his abdomen. Holy buckets!

A hunting companion had fired at what he mistook for a deer and hit Bryan instead. The mushrooming bullet had gone through the back of his right hand and the stock of his rifle. By then it was a shotgun blast of lead fragments and splinters of wood, which peppered his liver and shredded his right kidney. My heart squeezed cold in my chest. Bryan needed an operation, done expertly and promptly.

Dr. Ray Madison was a former medical school roommate and a trained surgeon. He had called the evening before from neighboring Koochiching, where he was staying while he also hunted deer. I telephoned his motel. Be there, Ray, please.

Ray and I began the operation an hour later, he still in his hunting boots. We scooped out bits of liver—a double handful lay loose in Bryan's belly—and removed the destroyed kidney. We placed drains of soft rubber, bringing them out through the skin, to facilitate seepage of toxins, old blood, and bile freed from its confining ducts by the wound. Things were dry and under control when we closed him up.

Bryan awoke from his anesthetic around midnight. "How are you?" I asked. My reflexes ran deep.

"Just fine, Doc," he mumbled.

Bile is devastating stuff to have dripping about in one's insides. In its proper place it digests food. Loose in the body, it does the same thing, but to structures nature holds dear. Bile drained out through all of Bryan's tubes, more seeped here and there. He eviscerated on the fifth day.

Evisceration is the total breakdown of an abdominal surgical wound. Few complications of surgery give patient, and physician, more anguish. Wound dressings suddenly bulge and loops of bowel pour out from beneath them into the forbidden realm of Outside.

I was on my own with this problem. I took Bryan back to the operating room, cleansed and replaced the bowel, tucked new drains into every nook and cranny I could invent. When I sewed him up again, I used great, tough sutures. For the next week I virtually lived in Bryan's room. Intravenous fluids. Antibiotic drugs. A fever chart with fanglike teeth: one night his temperature hit 106 degrees, the highest I have ever seen.

In my anxiety I prated, "How are you?"

"Just fine, Doc."

Toughness and courage, gleaned perhaps from those Viking ancestors.

Bryan became special. He survived, and he grinned at me a lot. We were friends, comrades who fought the fight together. I sent him to Duluth when he was stable enough to make the 165-mile trip. There he underwent three more operations to drain persistent pockets of bile.

Bryan and I still live in Northpine, so we meet once in a while. He grins easily, and when I ask him the Question he responds, "Just fine." He told me recently of two incidents that stick in his mind, these forty-some years later: how inexpensive the ambulance trip to Duluth was, and how provoked he had been there in our emergency room when I cut off his new undershorts. "They cost ninety-five cents, Doc. I'd just bought them at the Federated Store."

Bryan's Duluth surgeon was Randall LaVoy, a special friend and mentor. He told me, "That dang kid kept saying he was 'just fine.' Can you beat that?"

No sir, and neither has anyone else I've known.

Appendicitis

THE MOST COMMON emergency operation a non-specialist like myself performed was to remove an infected appendix. Appendicitis. The organ is a three- to four-inch-long pencil-shaped tube ending as a blind sac. Its attachment is to the last portion of the cecum, near where the small bowel enters it. Its narrow internal cavity communicates with the lumen of the cecum. Its function is debated, but it probably plays some role in immunity. Anatomists assure us that it is a nearly vestigial organ, one nature is in the process of eliminating. If it were not for its propensity to become infected, no one would give it a second thought.

By dint of necessity, appendicitis became a special interest of mine. For reasons I have never seen explained, appendicitis is less common these days than it was in the early days of my practice, when I would regularly see from fifteen to twenty cases a year. During the later years, three to five a year seemed the average.

There is only one treatment for appendicitis: removal of the appendix. Nowadays it is often done by laparoscope, an instrument inserted into the abdomen through inch-long incisions. For all my active years, it meant a standard incision in the right lower quadrant. An appendix dangling free is easy to remove, but if it is wrapped in scar and omentum, nature's remarkable intra-abdominal healing apron of tissue, or tucked into some obscure cranny where a respectable appendix would never consider hiding, the operation can cause a surgeon to sweat.

I reached the conclusion that appendicitis is occasionally an epidemic illness. Now before any of my colleagues jump up and down in outrage, let me offer some events to explain my theory. Twice I have had clustering of cases that defy chance. During one memorable month, I operated on nine people from Northpine, every one of whom had bona fide appendicitis, confirmed by tissue examination. Ray Constantine and his nephew Justin occupied one room of our hospital, their appendectomies a day apart. I learned subsequently that eight of the nine belonged to one of the local churches where a potluck supper had been served just before this "outbreak." On another occasion, I had a clustering of six cases in the span of ten days. Most remarkable of all, Carl, a wonderful older physician who worked with me for a couple of years, told of a family of four teenagers he had cared for. Every Thursday for four weeks, one of the youngsters turned up with pathologically proven appendicitis.

Todd Raymond was a burley trucker. He came to see me with symptoms that suggested appendicitis: pain in the right place, lack of appetite and nausea, tenderness when I prodded his abdomen. I put him in the hospital for a workup, but by late afternoon he seemed better. By morning he was his usual self and I sent him home. A month later, a repeat visit. Again the symptoms subsided over the next few hours. Todd agreed to have a suitable workup. A condition commonly mistaken for appendicitis is called Crohn's disease, or inflammatory bowel disease. I scheduled Todd to have a barium enema x-ray exam to rule out this condition. Our visiting radiologist called me to come and look at his films. In the lumen of the appendix, fortunately filled with gas that rendered it visible on the films, lay a densely opaque foreign body. We had no clue as to what it was, but it explained Todd's recurring symptoms.

I removed his appendix as an elective procedure. The pathologist identified the radio-opaque object as an amalgam tooth filling. When I explained this to Todd, he said, "Gosh, Doc, I didn't know you and the dentists were in cahoots." He was kidding. I think.

Jim Strongbody of Chippewa Lake was as nearly full-blooded Ojibwe as exists in these days, after the gene pooling provided by French and Scottish fur traders a couple of hundred years ago. Jim chose to live by the Old Ways: no rusted-out cars, no booze, tobacco as a religious aid instead of a demon ruling his life. His wife, Nancy, called me to their modest house one day when I had been at the reservation for my regular office hours.

Four bright-eyed, black-haired youngsters met me at the door. "Hello, Doctor," Birdie said and smiled shyly. "I took my medicine," piped up Margaret. Dustin poked his brother Myron and said, "Get out the way."

The Strongbodys had no electricity, their one concession to technology being kerosene lamps. By their pale yellow glow I groped my way alongside Jim's bed. The man was wiry strong, but on this night he looked like a mummy. Dehydration had dried the secretions of his mouth into gummy paste, and his gaunt cheeks were still fuller than his sunken eyes. He waved a hand at Nancy. "The can." He retched into it, his hands clutching an abdomen board-hard.

"How long?" I asked.

"Since three days," Nancy said softly, her speech graced by the singsong lilt that characterizes the Ojibwe language.

"You're very sick, Jim," I said. "I need to take you back to Northpine with me."

He said, "Give me *mushkeke*—medicine—Doc."

I shook my head. "The only medicine that will help you is an operation, and at once." When he started to object, I put on my dictator hat. "You are coming with me. No argument."

Jim mulled it over in his quiet way, then held out a hand to Nancy. She pulled him to a sitting position, and I saw his courage and fortitude. As we hobbled through his living room, he turned to the four wide-eyed youngsters and swiped at his eyes with the back of one hand. "Be good," he said.

At Northpine Hospital we prepared for surgery, but first we poured fluids, blood, and antibiotics into Jim. He lay stoically. About midnight I decided he was as ready as we could get him. I made a longer than usual incision in his right lower quadrant.

The stench of generalized bacterial peritonitis, the fetor that frenzied infection loose in the belly makes, is like nothing else I know. Sweetish, yet related to sewer gas, it can tighten the nostrils of the most hardened surgeon. We siphoned pus from Jim's abdomen by the pint. I searched for the appendix, found where it had been. Nothing remained but a ragged stump. We poured gallons of sterile salt water into the abdomen, draining it back into waste buckets. I placed flat rubber tubes, Penrose drains, into every cranny I could find.

For a week Jim Strongbody fought the gallant fight, all in the quiet of his inner spirit. I tried to prepare Nancy. She took my gestures with fortitude. We waited.

On the eighth day Jim passed the crisis. He went home three or four days later. He hobbled out to the county nurse's car, waiting to return him to the reservation, then suddenly turned, trudged painfully back to the hospital door where I watched, held out his hand, and said, "Thanks, Doc."

Oskar Jonason

BARBARA WAS SURGICAL NURSE for the day. I took sterile drapes from her and carefully isolated the operative area, leaving exposed a tense swelling in the old man's groin. A large, long-standing hernia, tolerated for so many years, had become a deadly threat when a loop of bowel twisted in the defect and locked itself firmly in place.

Oskar Jonason was a pastor. At ninety-one, his denomination considered him long retired, a status unacknowledged by Oskar. "I get mine orders from God," he explained. The man was clear mentally and in good enough physical shape that I felt confident the intestine was salvageable, although in need of prompt release from its lethal trap. I would use a local anesthetic, for at Oskar's age other forms of anesthesia would be more of a threat than the procedure. Carefully I injected lidocaine (Novocaine) into skin and tissues surrounding the bulging mass.

"Doctor," Oskar called from behind the shielding drape that hid his head from my view, "is it all right if I sing?"

"Why, yes. Unusual, but, certainly."

"Thank you." He cleared his throat experimentally.

Cacophony erupted. The ululating sound was bereft of melody. The term *atonal*, precise in describing what came from Oskar's throat, fell short, for musically it implies some degree of organization and predictability. How can one characterize the din? Hint at Native American song, mated with medieval chanting, inspired by a children's choir in a school for the deaf, rendered in a Norwegian accent inches thick.

"Our Lord and Savior," Oskar wailed, "it is good to talk to you today. What do You think I should share with these fine folks? Why don't I tell them about Northpine, located on such a beautiful lake. But then, You already know that. Lord, I wonder if I should let this young fellow know he is hurting me?

"Where was I? Oh yes, Northpine, found in the wilderness by those brave, pioneer spirits from Norway. Well, to be honest, God, there were a few rascals from Sweden, too. I'm not sure I understand why You didn't stop them. Ouch! He hurt me again, Lord. Maybe You should keep an eye on him. Guide his hand. We certainly hope he knows what he is doing down there. Oh, and Lord, he's a Scotchman. Well, You know best. I hope."

I'm grateful that masks are worn in surgery. Oskar seemed unaware of the odd glottal explosions and squeals leaking around them. Rarely can it be said, at the conclusion of an operation, that it was not only the patient who was in stitches.

Poachers, Arise!

I MAY HAVE INTIMATED in these stories that poaching was a "problem" in the country around Northpine, but many considered it to be an honorable profession. A lot depended on whether you got caught. Father Julian was the most successful poacher in the county, but he never came to grief because of it. Divine intervention? Maybe the fact that our game warden was Catholic had a little to do with his immunity. How could a fellow arrest his own priest? Father was so blatant, though. He would drive through town at high noon, deer legs sticking out of the trunk of his old Chevrolet Impala like hairy jackstraws.

I met him walking up from the lake one day, a brace of mallards in hand. "Self-defense," he told me. "They attacked. Vicious."

Joe Turner didn't have quite the same pull with the man upstairs. He was using a huge treble hook to snag walleyes one spring while they ran up Beaver Brook to spawn. Thing is, it wasn't walleye season yet, and, besides, you're not supposed to use such a direct method of catching them. He was sitting on the end of the exam table in the emergency room when I caught up with him, looking as sheepish as I ever saw that cocky son-of-a-gun. You see, one of the prongs of the great treble hook had penetrated his nasal septum and the rest was dangling in front of his lips. "Danged fish slipped off and that thing flew up like it was on a rubber band," he said. I tried not to laugh aloud. I failed.

Then there was Sven. He figured that since deer fed themselves at his expense—he farmed south of town—he had every right to feed off them when he felt like it. Schulyer French was warden then and, being a local boy himself, tended to look the other way if a hardscrabble farmer didn't rub his nose in the evidence. Sky was standing alongside Sven's pickup, doing his best not to see the dang deer legs sticking up out of its box, giving the lad a bit of fatherly advice, but Sven has always been on a short fuse. He revved up and drove smack over Sky's foot. Shot good-will halfway to Mars.

Locals called Abe Quick "Deerslayer." He was Northpine's second-most-celebrated poacher. Abe made his living off the land, grubby though that lifestyle might seem. To Abe, as with the padre, it was God's plan.

Deputy sheriff Mike Diensdorf brought Deerslayer to the emergency room that evening. Mike was as green around the gills as I had ever seen that unflappable man. Abe was a bear in build with broad shoulders and a belly sculpted by brew, his one concession to the virtues of society. He never washed himself or his clothing. His creed: "Show me another critter what owns a washing machine." Nature's law: no soap.

When I wheeled into the emergency room, Deerslayer was sitting up, hunched forward, left elbow on his knee, his right arm dangling. He held out his left hand and said, "Pardon me if I don't stand up." I shook it in a daze, my attention on his right shoulder.

An inch-thick stick of wood, a tree branch from its appearance, protruded from the front of Abe's right shoulder. I walked behind him. It emerged just lateral to his right shoulder blade. The man was impaled, through and through. And sitting upright. And talking. And extending the social courtesies.

I found a pulse and stroked his hand. "Feel this?"

"Sure, Doc."

The arm and hand were warm. Blood was getting down the extremity. I cut away Abe's shirt. No fresh bleeding, only ooze. Breathing sounds normal, no sign that it had penetrated the chest wall.

I asked, "How did this happen?"

"I fell out of a tree, one of them spruces with all the stubby, dead lower branches. Landed smack on one."

"Did it, uh, hang you up?" I shuddered at the image of Deerslayer dangling like a side of beef.

"Broke off. Had to walk a ways, though. Couldn't pull out that danged splinter."

I said, "I know better than to ask you what you were doing up that tree."

"Man's gotta live, Doc."

"I'll make arrangements for you to go to Duluth. Which hospital?"

He scowled at me. "What, go to Duluth? You're a doctor and this here's a hospital. You fix it."

"Abe, God only knows what that stick is lying against. I'm a country doctor—"

"'Course you are," he rumbled.

"You should have a surgeon take care of this."

"I ain't goin'. Besides, I can't afford no surgeon."

"But—"

"I'm gettin' kinda tired of this stick. Yank 'er out."

"Holy buckets."

Deerslayer declined general anesthesia. I ordered a dose of morphine and a little diazepam. Then I took a deep breath and pulled. Nothing. "Push from behind, Edna," I said to the nurse. The stick broke free. No fresh bleeding, only dark stuff bubbly with fat globules and old blood. I scrunched down and— I swear—for an instant I spied Edna's blue eye peering back at me through Deerslayer's shoulder.

Abe said, "Be danged."

After flushing the wound with gallons of sterile salt water, I placed rubber drains coming out from front and back. "Put him in Room Six," I said to Edna.

"Wait a minute, Doc. I ain't staying in the hospital."

"Yes you are, Abe."

"Come on."

"*Hospital!*"

"No danged hospital—"

"In the danged hospital or I'll shove that stick back where it was and send you down to Duluth."

Deerslayer considered. "Okay. Mike Diensdorf ain't still here, is he?"

I peeked out in the hall. "Waiting room."

"Want some venison, Doc? Got me a fine buck just before this happened."

"Chops?" I asked.

Special Delivery

I HAD COMPLETED A PROCEDURE in the operating room and sat in the doctors' lounge, the mouthpiece of a dictation machine at the ready. Record time.

From the hallway came the sound of running feet, always attention-grabbing in a hospital. The door burst open and nurse Edna Freeman poked her head around the jamb. She hollered, "Quick! Audrey Schneeweiss. Baby. Car. Parking lot."

I charged out of the hospital and nearly ran down a man whose frantic expression and wild gesticulations left little doubt that he was the father-to-be. "In the backseat, Doc," he shouted. "She's a havin' it! How could she *do* this to me?"

I threw open the door of his car to sight and sound of a woman in the last moments of labor. She lay supine across the seat, her skirt pulled onto her swollen abdomen. Even as I knelt in the opening, she groaned and began the final push of expulsion. The baby's head emerged smoothly. The woman continued her efforts. The shoulders, then the trunk, and finally the legs of a six- or seven-pound baby girl were born. Eyes open, arms raised in the startle position, the youngster swam around before me.

"Swam" because the amniotic sac, nature's transparent, fluid-filled sleeping bag for the unborn, remained intact, enclosing baby and liquid. This membrane is usually fragile enough so that the forces of labor or manipulations by impatient medics tear it by the time of actual delivery. A baby born "in the caul" is fairly rare today. In ages past it was considered a valuable omen that the child would have mystical powers.

My interest in the child's bent toward the occult was considerably less keen than a desire to see her breathe. I poked the sac with my index finger.

The baby blinked at me.

I poked with both index fingers. Vigorously.

A fluid wave vibrated the sac.

Beginning to feel mild anxiety, I essayed a series of jabs at the undulating bag of waters.

The baby scowled at me.

Suddenly I was more than anxious. Poking, frantic scratching, pinching, and picking with my nails did not rupture that hideously tough membrane. In a scrub suit with no sharp implement—Wait! Action followed inspiration. I nipped the amniotic sac with my front teeth and a gush of warm, salty water cascaded into my face and down my front.

Girl Schneeweiss bleated in annoyance. Warming to her task, she screamed baby imprecations in my ear. By now, Edna had arrived, burdened with supplies. I clamped the umbilical cord and wrapped the child in a blanket. Holding her in my arms, I backed out of the car while nurses transferred Audrey to a wheeled cart.

We marched triumphantly into the hospital, a procession. Properly, Northpine's newest princess, with me as her escort, led the way. Art Carlson, a courtier in janitorial jeans, cleared the path, holding doors deferentially. Maids in waiting in nursing white scurried about, oohing and ahing. The Queen Mother, dazed but happy, was jostled along on her portable throne.

Dashing from front to back of the parade, fluttering like a certain Prokofievian bird, came the new father.

I heard him myself.

"She did it. She did it! She went ahead and *did* it!"

Some days are like that.

God Calling

FOR ALL THE YEARS of my frontline practice, fishing was my escape. I reasoned that if I managed to clear my back porch without the telephone ringing, I could with pristine conscience disappear for a few precious hours onto lake or stream. Getting away for a break became an obsession.

For a while we owned a cabin—one in constant need of repair—at a lake some thirty miles from Northpine. We had once elected to spend a week at this hideaway. The water pipes into the kitchen were in their usual state of non-function when we arrived. I crawled as far under the cabin as I could and was sizing up the situation from my vantage of no plumbing skills whatsoever when there came sounds of someone crawling after me. Flat prone, with no room to turn over, I heard a masculine voice say, "That you, Doc? Tex, down the road, saw you drive by and, see, I got this pain here in my belly. Thought maybe you should take a look." I confess that my impulse was to kick when my foot fetched up against the guy's head, but I inched past him.

Out in the sun, on the sand that was our yard, I asked him my questions, prodded his belly, found clear evidence of appendicitis. Our "vacation" lasted two-and-a-half hours, for when I went back to Northpine to operate, Barbara insisted on returning, too. If I had been asked to rate her mood, I would put it at forty-five below zero. Or more. We decided a "vacation" was too much work.

· · ·

We Northpiners wryly called Labor Day "Liberation Day." By afternoon, a stream of cars towing boats clogged the highway heading south. It's not that we didn't enjoy having summer visitors come to our town. Their diversity enriched us socially and intellectually, and meeting their needs was the basis of our economy. It's just that we got tired.

One fall, Labor Day came along and I happily headed for my favorite trout stream. The day was September-warm, the skies clear and blue, the stream murmuring at me in that special language requiring time and study to translate. I felt strain and tension melt off me like icicles caught in the sun. To make it perfect, the fish were biting and I had caught four beauties.

When one is standing in the bed of a lively stream, its music is all one hears. I was rapt, listening to its cadenzas, when I heard what I thought was a voice, faint as a half-remembered dream. "Doctor MacDonald," it sang. I blinked. Had I fallen asleep in the arms of such tranquility? I shrugged and drifted a line past a promising ripple. "Doctor MacDonald." Again? Good Lord, is this what hallucinations are like? All still now. A shiver.

I returned my attention to the stream. "Doctor MacDonald!" Petulant. Demanding. This time I could not shrug it off. I confess, even as I blush to admit it, that I said out loud, "Is that you, God? Were those Old Testament guys telling the truth about what they claimed to have heard?"

It came again, directionless in the rush of water about me. It had to be some principle of physics rather than of psychiatry or theology. I clambered up the bank of my beloved stream. The sound came from the road, where my car was parked. Real. An electronically amplified bullhorn.

Highway patrolman Tim Nelson stood beside my car. "Bad accident, Doc. Hospital."

We roared back to Northpine in tandem, I trying to keep up with Tim. At the hospital I found mayhem.

A van holding eleven young adults, counselors at a camp nearby, had rolled over. One youth was dead, the other ten injured severely. The driver had been trapped under debris and hot radiator liquid had cascaded over her, inflicting deep burns. She and each of the others had sustained multiple fractures.

It happened that an old friend, a retiree, as well as one of my medical school professors were each vacationing in the area. Somehow people at the hospital had located them. They had rolled up their sleeves and were working like troupers. We three spent the afternoon and half the night coping with the injuries, stabilizing and reducing fractures, treating burns. Our diminutive hospital was filled. Off-duty nurses returned, and we managed. No one else succumbed, and the driver, the most seriously hurt, eventually recovered. Fortunately, as it turned out, no fishing hideaway is too remote.

I found my fly rod and four mummified fish in the trunk of my car just before Christmas.

Are Country Doctors Born, Not Made?

A COUNTRY DOCTOR: the phrase conjures images of kindly grandpa-types, perhaps more empathetic than up-to-date. Whatever validity that model might have had vanished before my time. My colleagues, those special friends who also know the responsibility of practicing medicine hours from help by a full cadre of specialists, and I are held to the same standards as are city physicians in their multitudes.

Learned colleagues who became friends while I taught at the University of Minnesota occasionally expressed awe that anyone would relish frontline medicine. Forty percent of the citizens of our grand state live outside a metropolitan area. Rural. Far fewer than forty percent of the state's physicians live among them. Alone or in groups of three or five, miles and hours from the comforting aid of specialists, we who chose such a life often faced situations for which we were not prepared. A necessity for a rural physician is knowledge of oneself and one's limitations and a willingness to refer, no matter how inconvenient. Still, situations arose when there was no time to move a patient. What then? Read a resource book, call a distant colleague for advice, even pray for a moment—then square one's shoulders and do what must be done. It is amazing what one can do when there is absolutely no alternative.

One must also factor in fatigue. For twenty-two years I was the only physician available for emergencies. An all-night session at the hospital led to the usual full day in the office. Vacations were brief, fill-in doctors unavailable. I once calculated (at 3:00 A.M., while I awaited the arrival of an unborn baby who seemed content to remain where he was) that I had been on emergency call more than 10,000 nights of my life.

If I could identify the mainspring of my love for the profession of medicine, I believe it is the chance to be involved in the life of my community. The art of medicine involves more than knowledge of symptoms, conditions, and treatments. One must be sensitive to the unspoken message each person brings to the office, for a patient is always apprehensive. Empathy is crucial, and, I suspect, doctors who lack it fuel the rumbling discontent I sometimes hear directed at my beloved craft.

Yet within the very attempt to console someone there lies a trap, for above all else a physician must be a *scientist*. The schism separating scientific thought from the rest of human endeavor can be almost unbridgeable in the hustle of a busy practice. How does one cope with the latest medical fad advanced by a patient? ("Doctor, do you believe in hypoglycemia?") As though it were a religious statement. I try to explain the facts as a scientist must view them, but frequently I lose the attention and sometimes the respect of my patient. Unfortunately, science cares little for testimonial evidence.

Adequate medical care is a right. Ensuring that every citizen has access to it creates committees in Congress and turmoil on the home front. I hear that too many physicians are being graduated today, that mal-distribution is to blame for an enduring shortage of country doctors. A few educators have tried to address this issue.

The Rural Physician Associate Program (affectionately

known as R-PAP), managed by the University of Minnesota Medical School, is the brainchild of Dr. John Verby, M.D. Begun in 1970, this innovative curriculum places third-year medical students under the tutorship of selected practitioners in rural communities all around Minnesota. The student receives academic credit and stays for nine to twelve months. The program continues to fulfill its promise today under the direction of Dr. Walter Swentko, M.D.

A crowning highlight of my own professional career was an opportunity to be involved in R-PAP, first as a rural physician, then as associate director of the program. I served as preceptor for seven students over the same number of years, and I learned as much as I taught, thanks to bright inquisitive young people named David, David, John, Dennie, Mike, Steve, and Mike. Not only does R-PAP prove to be a valuable educational opportunity, it also has the salutary effect of persuading many a city-bred student (and his or her spouse) that a good life exists away from the hum of a large city. Two of my former students eventually returned to Northpine to join me in practice. R-PAP was—and continues to be—a success.

All things come to an end, and so have these tales. In my vanity I have considered myself a pioneer, but truth, with its uncompromising morality, forces me to acknowledge that I followed in the footsteps of others. Like a tide creeping up some beach, each succeeding wave obliterates the record of that which came before, writing proudly on its sand as though it were immortal, heedless of the wave gathering just behind it.

Northpine. A community small enough that we who live here can know each other, person-to-person, yet large enough to accommodate the gifts and passions of all. I am not unique, nor is my beloved Northpine a one-and-only. I pray that my words will light a spark of empathy among my rural colleagues. In a sense, I hope that I speak for all of us.

I love the north country and cannot always fathom my good fortune in having found my way here, of living among those for whom my respect and affection are as great as that inland sea known as Lake Superior. We who love it cannot leave for long before its majesty draws us back.

And so it is with the people of the north.

About the Author

ROGER A. MACDONALD, M.D., was a rural physician from 1948 to 1980, when he became associate director of the Rural Physician Associate Program at the University of Minnesota Medical School. Now retired, he divides his time between Grand Marais, Minnesota, and La Verne, California. *A Country Doctor's Casebook* is his first book.

A Country Doctor's Casebook was designed and set in type by Chris Long at Mighty Media, Minneapolis. The typefaces are Vendetta and Triplex Italic, both designed by John Downer. Printed by Maple-Vail Book Manufacturing Group.